M000282987

UNLOCKING THE GOLDEN HANDCUFFS

Leaving the Public Service for Work You Really Love

Lewis S. Eisen

COPYRIGHT INFORMATION

CATALOGING IN PUBLICATION DATA

Eisen, Lewis S., 1957–
    Unlocking the Golden Handcuffs

ISBN: 978-1-988749-03-7   paperback

1. Business and Economics—Careers/General. 2. Business and Economics—Government and Business. 3. Business and Economics—Careers/Job Hunting.

Vers. 1.1

DEDICATION

To all my former public service colleagues who dream of leaving the nest but have never tried their wings.

Make all the excuses you want—the economy, your kids, your lack of a degree, your lousy boss, the transmission on your car—but don't fool yourself. A pivot that never starts was blocked by one thing, and one thing only: being afraid.

~ Adam Markel, *Pivot* [1]

[1] Adam Markel: Pivot: The Art and Science of Reinventing Your Career and Life (2016), Atria Books

ACKNOWLEDGEMENTS

Special thanks to Fern Lebo, co-author of the forthcoming book *The Talent Revolution,* for her editing. As the author of a number of business books of her own, Fern ensures a modernity to my writing style.

Thanks also to Joyce Eisen and Michèle Colyer for their editorial contributions and comments around messaging. Thanks to them, this book tries to sustain an uplifting tone throughout.

Finally, much appreciation to my mentor, Adam Markel, the author of *Pivot: The Art and Science of Reinventing Your Career and Life,* who's supported me during my own transition out of the public service and back into the work I truly love: training, speaking, and writing.

CONTENTS

Chapter 1

GETTING UNSTUCK

This book is my offer of encouragement to every public servant who finds their job to be less than fully rewarding.

My goal is to show you that you can have it better. Your job skills are in demand in the private sector and lots of good opportunities are available for the taking. If you want it, you can have a truly fulfilling career doing work you really love to do. You'll see the opportunities available to you when you begin to open your mind to the possibilities.

Breaking free of the public service starts with a change in attitude. It starts by recognizing when you're stuck.

✧ Frank ✧

Detective Frank Simmons (not his real name) has been working for the police department of a large city for 25 years.

The early years were exciting; he was learning the ropes, the players, the game...everything he needed to move up the ranks. The job promised the usual rewards: security, possibility of career advancement, lots of training, and so on.

Frank tried his hand in different sections of the force, gaining broad experience to make himself an attractive candidate for a management position. He genuinely enjoyed his early years working as a constable and eventually moved up to detective. He saw the good and the bad in the operations of the force, and did his best to be a good team player.

Frank isn't lazy by any means, and he believes in an honest day's work for an honest dollar. Over the years he worked those honest days, plus others. He pitched in to help when there were personnel shortages in other units, and he compliantly put in overtime hours when the need arose. On more than one occasion his vacation was cancelled or postponed at the last minute due to "operational requirements." But Frank understood that that was the nature of the beast; people working in emergency services need to be available when duty calls.

Over time, Frank applied for a number of more senior positions as they opened up. After all, he thought, the closer to the top of the ladder he could be, the more opportunity he would have to fix some of the pieces that were broken. The morale of the force had been steadily declining for a number of years, and Frank wanted to make the police force a better place to work for both management and employees. That achievement would have been both professionally and personally satisfying.

While theoretically autonomous, Frank's police force is run by a branch of the government. The "broken" pieces of the police force are situations that most workers in public service positions encounter every day:

▸ a cumbersome bureaucracy, bottlenecked at the top
▸ a lack of employee recognition
▸ a toxic work environment and depressed employee morale
▸ an unbridled waste of public funds, and
▸ the repeated promotion of unsuitable people into senior positions.

These problems aren't new by any means, and you've most likely heard of them. What's of note, however, is that government as a workplace doesn't seem to be getting any better over time, and Frank's police force was a typical instance of that stagnancy. After a number of years had passed with no improvement in the situation, he realized that change was going to be harder than he thought.

His younger self would have picked up the challenge and charged ahead to tame as many wild horses as he could. Today he's no longer his younger self. Years of thanklessly working both paid and unpaid overtime, following absurdly over-complicated internal procedures, and watching many less-qualified colleagues being given undeserved promotions had drained the fire out of him. After a while he became too weary even to challenge the system, much less fix it.

Frank had always hoped he would have the kind of job where he could push himself hard while enjoying the work and then reaping the rewards at the end of the day. This police force was not that, nor was it going to become that in the foreseeable future.

Despite his frustration and unhappiness at work, Frank stays put. He feels stuck.

"Twenty years ago [before a major internal restructuring] the force was a great place to work," he says. "It's sure not like that today."

"Why don't you leave and find something better?" I ask periodically.

"I can't afford to," is always the reply. "I'll lose my pension and my benefits. I won't have the security. And what would I do anyway?" Not waiting for an answer, he'd continue, "No, I'll just wait out the 12 – 11 – 10 – 9... etc. years remaining before I can collect my pension."

Frank has resigned himself to working more years in a bad job. He sees no way out.

✧ Freda ✧

"But I like my job!" Freda Dumont (not her real name) protested, right after I suggested that she might want to think about working somewhere other than government.

"Really?" I asked. "Do you love your job, or just not hate it?"

Freda paused briefly to think. "You're right," she conceded. "I don't hate it."

"The people here are great!" she added quickly.

She's right about that. The people working in the government are, by-and-large, genuinely great people. They are intelligent, capable, well-intentioned, hard-working, honest, and friendly. Many of them are creative, highly insightful, über-skilled, and work their buns off.

For the most part during my 15 years in the public service I worked with some stellar people and—despite the odd noteworthy exception—I grew to respect them as professionals and as colleagues. As I moved from one office to another I was sad to leave them. I still miss working with many of them; they were great people.

But here's a shocking thought: loving the people you work with is not the same as loving your work.

Loving the people you work with comes from shared experience, collegiality, and mutual respect. The same way soldiers in an army unit bond together while fighting a battle, you bond with your co-workers as you face the office obstacles.

Make no mistake, though: working with other good soldiers doesn't make fighting a pleasant experience. If you are staying in your current position solely because you love the people you work with, you may be settling to stick with a bad situation for the wrong reasons. As was Freda.

"So why don't you find a job you really love?" I asked her. "Wouldn't that be more rewarding?"

> Loving the people you work with
> is not the same as loving your work

"It will get better here," she responded optimistically. "Things are changing around here."

I've met hundreds of Franks and Fredas, all of whom suffer from the same problem: although they want good, rewarding employment, they are held prisoner within the civil service because they have adopted a set of beliefs that act as barriers to career change.

Along with those beliefs, they have made assumptions about work life in the outside world based on nothing more than their own experience inside government. The public service itself does nothing to dispel these beliefs or assumptions.

Together, these beliefs, assumptions, and the public service psyche comprise the golden handcuffs. They virtually hold people prisoner in an unhappy work life.

I love Freda's hopefulness in the face of a troubled future. I don't share her optimism.

Some People Love Working There

Don't get me wrong. I'm not suggesting that the entire public service is unhappy. Many, many people spend long, rewarding careers in the civil service spanning several decades, and they retire feeling well-rewarded for their labours and satisfied with their accomplishments.

My hat is off to these people! They clearly found their life's work and grew with it. The public service was good to them, and they took advantage of the many experiences it has to offer.

But Too Many Don't

Sadly, these individuals number all too few. Far too many people who work in the government are unhappy, frustrated, or just plain defeated.

This situation as I describe it might seem strange to people in the outside world. To most eyes, the public service seems like an enviable place to work: a steady job, good pay, an employer who won't go bankrupt (in most cases), and lots of powerful unions to fight your battles. It seems ideal, doesn't it? Indeed, the public service has some very plum jobs, at very attractive salaries. In many cases, the salary range is higher than what you find in private industry. What more could an employee want?

Because of this public perception, any negative complaints about work life in the public service tend to be interpreted as griping by unappreciative employees. That position has been echoed by at least one media commentator who wondered aloud why federal govern-ment employees—who get great benefits and can't be fired—are so much unhappier in their jobs than private-sector workers?

To be fair, the public service has no monopoly on people who are unhappy at work. A 2016 survey of employees reported in the Canadian HR Reporter reveals that almost one-half of professionals are unhappy in their jobs.[2]

It's no different in the United States. Forbes reported a Gallup poll finding that happy employees are outnumbered 2:1 by unhappy ones.[3] The poll discovered that 63% of employees are "not engaged," meaning they are unhappy at work but not drastically so.

The Powerful Versus the Powerless

From where I sit, it seems that the proportion of individuals who are happy working in the public service grows as they ascend the organizational pyramid. The highest-level civil servants are the best remunerated, have the most power and influence, leave the largest footprints, and have the greatest amount of job satisfaction. In contrast, the lower you sit on the ladder, the

[2] Unhappy at work: http://www.hrreporter.com/article/27461-one-half-of-working-population-unhappy-in-job-survey/

[3] Forbes: https://www.forbes.com/sites/susanadams/2013/10/10/unhappy-employees-outnumber-happy-ones-by-two-to-one-worldwide/#4f234d7362a6

less you are paid, the less power and influence you have, and the less your contribution is noticed.

For that reason, people caught in the civil service have come to believe that the only way to make life better for themselves is to try to move up through the ranks. They apply to one job competition after another, hoping to achieve a higher job classification, earn more money, and sit in the company of more people with more power.

For some people, for sure, moving up the public service ladder is exactly the right career move for them. They are destined to become the top dogs in their departments. If you are one of those people, you can stop reading this handbook now. Congratulations! You are in the right place. You have found work you love.

But for everyone else, moving up the chain is slow and arduous. While one moves to higher classified positions, the order of magnitude of responsibility grows while the job satisfaction may not. Many of those people would switch careers in an instant if they found one in a field they loved while being able to keep all the salary, benefits, and job security of the civil service job.

And yet they stay. Why?

The Golden Handcuffs

What are these handcuffs that hold unhappy public servants in place, afraid to look for truly rewarding work in the outside world?

Actually, they relate to a number of areas.

- ✦ some are financial, where the employee feels bound to a rich compensation, benefits, or pension arrangement

- ✦ some are skill related, based on the employee's own projection of the usefulness of their skills in the open market

- ✦ some of them are based on the comfort afforded by working in a unionized environment, such as the ability to grieve and to bargain collectively;

- ✦ some of them are based simply on pervasive assumptions, such as the common view that job security lies in the demand for the activity you do rather than for the skills you have.

Because of these beliefs, Franks and Fredas working in government stay put. Despite being unhappy with their jobs and wanting something better, they are not going anywhere, both literally and figuratively. They are stuck in the civil service and see no way to transition to a more rewarding work experience.

Learning About the Real World

These handcuffs may be self-imposed, but they still have a firm hold. That hold is compounded significantly by a general lack of knowledge among civil servants about what aspects can be very different in the private sector.

Government is an artificial construct, powered by politics and philosophies rather than by sound business principles. The workplace outside government is what I call the Real World—where things operate on a different basis.

In the Real World, skills like creativity, originality, and resourcefulness are considered assets, not inconveniences, to management. Some things that are broken in government don't exist out in the Real World. If you knew about them, you might be tempted to look outside the bubble of the public service and see what you can accomplish.

There is Hope

The purpose of this book is to teach you about how working in the Real World can be very different from the public service.

At a time when Canada's unemployment rate is conspic-uously low[4], it's unconscionable that so many public servants are frustrated or unhappy at their work.

If you are one of these people, then take heart. This book is for you. There's no reason you should have to stay where you are and suffer the indignity of a less than stellar job or career. Perhaps something in the chapters that follow will help you pivot on your path, and redirect it to a more satisfying work life.

This handbook is for all the government colleagues I worked with over the years, who have suffered under systemically poor management—ironically, all under a continuous series of new initiatives to improve manage-ment. This is for those who have experienced unfair treatment around job promotion, all in the name of "fairness." This is for those who know that they have within themselves the competencies, experience, and energy to perform at a high level, but are held back by rigid job classifications and a system that values process over results. This is for all of you who would like to move on to something better but don't know how or where to start.

---

[4] The Star: Canada's unemployment rate falls to lowest in nearly nine years

Contents

Here's how we will proceed. In chapter 2, we look at what it means to truly love your work.

In chapter 3 we examine a number of myths and assumptions about work and career that are incorrect. In general I have found these myths pervasive in the public service. We're going to bring them out into the open and dispel them.

Chapter 4 explains some of the factors that cause the public service to operate differently from the Real World. If you've worked solely in the public service all your life, then you may not realize that these factors affect how your current job works.

From there, we begin a set of chapters examining how jobs and careers function differently out in the Real World, and why that difference can operate to your advantage. We'll cover career advancement, desirable job skills, job interviews, delegation, staffing, projects, job security, leadership, and bureaucracy. As you go through these chapters, you may discover that much of what you know about the way organizations operate is in fact only applicable to the civil service, and that things are very different in the Real World. For some of these areas, there's no reason government couldn't operate the same way if it wanted to, but there needs to be a lot of change before that happens.

In chapters 12 and 13 we examine the reasons you might raise in a knee-jerk reaction to the thought of leaving your current situation, no matter how bad it might be. Some of these reasons are intellectual and some of them are emotional. Just as we did with the myths, we're going to bring them out into the open so we can challenge them.

The final chapter looks at what you need to do to begin making the transition from public service to private sector, and recommends some resources that might help you explore the possibilities.

Sources

The people and their stories captured in this book are real. The examples are pulled from governments at all levels: federal, state/provincial, and municipal. In many cases the sources asked for anonymity, fearing that speaking the truth about their workplace would bring about reprisal of some kind.

I acknowledge their courage and thank them for allowing me to tell their stories.

Web Site

This book was written with a companion Web site at **goldenhandcuffs.net**, where you can find hyperlinks to many of the sources that appear in the footnotes.

In addition, you will find links to various resources that can help you as you explore the world outside the civil service.

Chapter 2

WHAT IT MEANS TO LOVE YOUR WORK

Passion is energy. Feel the power that comes from focusing on what excites you."

~ Oprah Winfrey

L oving your work is about professional and personal satisfaction. It's about reaping the rewards that are most important to you.

Here are some examples of people who love their work. The work is different in each case, but what they all have in common is that they love more than the paycheque arriving at the end of the day. The work itself provides the rewards.

✧ Mike ✧

Mike Hovey didn't grow up dreaming that he would be a firefighter. He liked cars, building things, and doing home renovations. But he just hated his previous job. It was totally unfulfilling.

"I wanted to get the most out of life," he explains. "I wasn't happy going in to work five days a week, from 9AM to 5PM, working a job where I couldn't take any pride in my work."

His career took a sudden turn after a particularly bad episode with one employer, and he's never looked back since then. For the last five years he has worked in the fire department of a major urban centre.

Most of us know firefighting as difficult and dangerous work, and Mike agrees with that characterization. Nonetheless, he loves his work.

"I get to show up on someone's worst day and try to make a difference in their life," he says contentedly.

"Whether it's extricating someone from a crushed car in an accident or consoling a distraught family member, I get to feel real pride in my achievements. Every day on the job is like that, even if we're just bringing kids through the station and showing them the fire trucks."

One of the things Mike hated about his old job was that they were always trying to cut corners.

"Quality was less important than costs and deadlines," he recalls. "There was no pride in workmanship."

Mike understands the forces that drive him.

"I'm a workhorse," he admits. "I thrive on achievement. I like accomplishment. I enjoy challenging myself. I don't want to sit around doing nothing. I want to look back at every single job and say that I feel good that I did good work."

"We are never asked to cut corners in this job," he says. "We do what we have to, to get the job done. This job is 100% about the results."

✧ Rob ✧

Rob Lagana has been running a personal training business for 25 years. His specialty is helping women in their 30s, 40s, and 50s transform their bodies through a combination of exercise and nutrition. His approach is holistic: mind, body, and spirit. He loves his work.

"I can make a real difference in people's lives," he says. I can see their self-esteem go up as we progress, and the change in the way they feel about themselves. I love seeing my clients succeed. That's the best reward."

Rob knows what factors drive him. "I've always been passionate about fitness and health," he says. "I see a lot of misinformation out there and a lot of people trying to make a buck from unsophisticated clients. I've done the research, and I know which exercise and nutrition practices are backed by science and which ones are gimmicks. I want to help as many people as possible become healthy the right way, the safe way."

✧ Maya ✧

Maya Lightfoot also works in the health and wellness space. She's a Health Promotion Specialist serving employees of a large government department, teaching people skills that improve both their work life and home life. She covers a range of topics, from how to eat properly to how to manage anger and stress, and how to aid someone in distress or at risk for suicide.

She loves her work.

"The information I provide in my course helps make people's lives better," she explains, "and they really want to learn about what I have to tell them. Everyone takes away something different from my sessions."

"I get to share my knowledge and experience in a field I'm passionate about." Maya's work is both professionally and personally rewarding, and her job satisfaction is evident.

"What really makes my work gratifying is receiving so much positive feedback after the course from people on the improvement in the quality of their lives. I know that I'm making a difference."

Although she's not a public servant, she works alongside other public servants and sees what they have to go through.

"I'm so glad I'm independent," she admits. "I don't have to put up with any of the crap that they do: the bureaucracy, the union, the way everything simple has to become so complicated. I have all the benefits of the career without having to put up with the nonsense."

Maya recognizes that she's in a fortunate position. "Having a certain amount of independence means a great deal to me. I'm a professional, and I'm working like a professional. It's very rewarding."

✧ Lewis ✧

Yep, that's me.

As part of my training and consulting practice, for many years I travelled around the United States and Canada giving one day courses, teaching lawyers and other professionals how to use technology effectively and productively.

Having left the public service, I'm back doing that again. I run workshops on how to write administrative policies properly, so that they're clear, succinct, and respectful to the people they govern. And I love my work.

I love running workshops and courses. I love planning them, I love preparing for them, I love practising the patter. I get a real thrill from standing in front of the classroom and leading the group through the process of learning—going from confusion to clarity.

Professionally, my mission is to make difficult content easy to understand, and no matter what I'm teaching, I love doing it.

Sure, there are good days and there are bad days, and there are easy times and there are difficult times. But teaching a course in my field fulfills me personally, professionally, academically, and emotionally, and whenever I have the opportunity to do that I love going to work.

So what exactly does it take to be able to love your work? Loving the people you work with can be a big part of it, but as mentioned before, that's not the same as loving the work itself.

Loving the Results

Some people love their work because they love the results of the work. Mike, Rob, and Maya's love for their work is directly related to the rewards they receive as part of that work.

For me, I am a teacher at heart. I have always been a teacher, no matter what my profession was at the time. I love explaining things to people, making difficult and complex concepts sound easy and simple. My reward is having people tell me that now they understand. The reward is real and the benefit is real. It's a win-win situation for both sides.

Loving your activities

Some people love their work because they love the activities associated with their work.

Throughout the day you engage in various activities connected with your work. Those activities could be anything from speaking, listening, reading, discussing, analyzing, calculating, testing, troubleshooting, problem-solving...the list could on and on. If you love performing these activities, then are more likely to love your work.

But be careful here: your work involves not only the primary activities that are part of your job description, but also the secondary activities that must be done to support the primary activities. Secondary activities could be anything from attending meetings, filing documents, writing reports, to photocopying and stapling paper.

If you don't enjoy those secondary activities, that's certainly understandable. No job is 100% free of drudge work. What you need to ensure is that the non-enjoyable activities don't take a disproportionate amount of your time. When that starts to happen, your work enjoyment goes out of balance.

A Matter of Proportion

Granted no work is perfect. Every work has pluses and minuses, and the pluses should obviously outweigh the minuses. What I have found among people working in the public service is a particularly low threshold for this ratio, sometimes as low as 50/50 or less. Expectations have fallen so low that the job is considered good if 50% of it is good.

Fifty percent? No wonder you're unhappy!

Fifty percent is not enough. Would you continue to attend a season of ticketed events—sports, music, theatre, or whatever—if 50% of what you attended was bad? Would you continue to eat at a restaurant where 50% of the time the meal was not acceptable? Would you continue to have a friend over for drinks and conversation if 50% of the time was not enjoyable? I don't think so.

You are entitled to better. There's no reason that you shouldn't be able to enjoy 80%, 90%, or more of your work.

The Importance of Environment

When you are trained in a specific field like economics, health, accounting, and so on, then finding a job in that field is usually a good fit—but not always. Sometimes the work is right but the setting is wrong, for example, where the work environment is toxic.

Even with the right job or career, it's difficult to love your work in a toxic work environment. You dread going there in the morning, you are stressed throughout the day, and you are drained when you leave for home. It's soul-drowning at best, and heart-attack-inducing at worst.

It's no secret that many government offices are less than stellar work environments. I've encountered some horrible office colleagues. I had an Executive Director who outright lied to his subordinates, subordinates who were out to backstab anyone who got in their way, and peers who couldn't spell the word *cooperation* if their lives depended on it. There are some nasty work environments.

> # Good job + toxic environment = bad job

"It's perpetually demoralizing," says one former public servant. "It feels like no matter what you do, nothing ever changes."

But hold on a minute here! Can't a toxic work environment happen anywhere? Government offices have no monopoly on bad corporate culture. Aren't you just as likely to find horrible people working in any work environment?

Yes, of course! Many work environments outside of government are just as dysfunctional if not more so. That doesn't change the equation.

If you are working in a toxic environment—be it public service or private sector—get out as soon as you can. You'll be much happier for it.

Finding That Right Fit

That's the tough part, for sure.

Maybe you love helping people. Maybe you love working with animals or children. Maybe you love music or design or food or travel or...the list of environments could go on and on.

Maybe you love being creative or inventive. Maybe you love meeting new people. Maybe you love building things—or smashing them down. Maybe you love reading or writing or talking or listening...the list of activities could also go on and on.

Whatever does it for you, I want you to imagine what it might be like if you could do that as your life's work. Just take a moment to imagine it.

Do you love buying clothes or jewelry? What if you could do that as your life's work and get paid for it? Do you love hosting people for dinner? Do you love driving down a country road? What if you could do whatever you loved as your life's work and earn your salary at the same time? Wouldn't that be wonderful?

If you loved your work, you'd look forward to each day with relish. You'd be a nicer person to be around. You wouldn't carry your anger or frustration home to your family, or take it out on some innocent shopkeeper or bus driver who gets in your way at the wrong moment.

If you don't know now what exactly it is that you would love doing, that's okay. You don't have to decide today.

It may take you a long while to figure out what it is that will bring you the reward that a good career should.

On this book's companion Web site you'll find a number of links to resources that can help you in that area—whenever you're ready.

All you need to do for now is open your mind to the possibilities.

Links to sources and other
resources are available on the
Unlocking the Golden Handcuffs web site
www.goldenhandcuffs.net/

Chapter 3

DISPELLING SOME MYTHS

Unlocking the golden handcuffs will take us several steps. We will start by dispelling five myths that most people have about working a job. I myself believed some of these myths to be truths for many years, until I learned better.

Some of these myths may be so engrained in your thinking that you may not realize it. They are reflective of prevailing attitudes. Even if you never heard anyone make these statements aloud, you would have been expected to adopt them as premises or foundational statements to account for the activities and attitudes that accompany them. The fact that the statements remain unspoken is what gives them their longevity. Were they to be actually uttered aloud, they would be open to challenge.

These myths can be found in many work environments, as well as home environments. They may be vestiges of your upbringing, or something that you have encountered in the workplace. I have found these myths to be especially pervasive in the civil service. They form the public service "culture," and need to be exposed so that they can be challenged.

If you've only had exposure to the civil service in your work career, it might never occur to you that these beliefs might not be true. Until we dispel them, you will continue to assume that they are a reflection of the way the world works. So let's knock them off one at a time.

Myth #1: The for-profit sector is less honourable than the not-for-profit sector

One of the things that most surprised me when I started to work with the public service was the number of people who think that *profit* is a dirty word.

For these people, an individual or organization that wants to make a profit is somehow doing a "bad" thing. I'd go so far as to say that there's a faint but distinctly noticeable air of superiority among public servants, based on a notion that working in the government is a nobler calling than working in the for-profit world.

It's an odd mindset, almost as if all the for-profit enter-prises in the world are corrupted by the allure of greed. Big companies, small companies, consultants... anyone who's charging the government an amount equal to more than their direct expenses is painted with the same brush. The characterization "out to make a profit" is spoken with the same disdain one might use when saying "beats helpless puppies."

If you are one of those people who believes that working for profit is bad, then you need to step back and ask yourself where that belief comes from.

Yes, it's true that when one's goal is to make a profit, one has different decision-making parameters than one does when the goal is something else.

And yes, it's also true that where profit is the **sole** goal of an organization or individual, they might sacrifice other values that we consider important.

Practically speaking, though, an enterprise that is totally profit obsessed to the exclusion of all else can't survive very long. The longest standing companies in most industries are those that also promote ideals like employee welfare, customer satisfaction, safety, security, research and development, ecological preservation, and similar values that are aimed at bettering the lives of people.

But even if an organization doesn't adopt any of the altruistic, socially expected values that consumers look

Profit is not a dirty word!

for, the for-profit operating model has a lot of merit. Many, many people benefit from it.

Take a simple example like a manufacturer of canned tomatoes. Yes, the business is in it for profit, and yes, it tries to fetch the highest price it can.

But there's nothing sinister about that. The sale will succeed only when it delivers sufficient value to the purchaser. Moreover, it's the purchaser who decides when the value is sufficient, not the vendor.

It might be tempting for you to do a quick mental calculation, estimating the value of the tomatoes and the cost of the aluminum in the can. But it's short-sighted to add those two amounts together and then conclude that any price charged above that produces profit for the vendor.

Most vendors' costs are hidden from us. The manufacturer pays money for service to many people, all of whom work hard: the farmer who harvests the tomatoes, the trucker who takes them to the factory, the metal maker who produces the can, the artist who designs the label, the technicians who operate the machines that put the labels on, the packers and drivers who ship the product to the stores, and the clerks in the stores who sell it to us. All of these people along the way are putting in an honest day's work and need to be paid from the same pie.

These people aren't money-grabbing scoundrels. They're all workers just like you and me, all trying to earn enough money to feed and clothe their families, send their children to nice schools and buy them nice things, and try to squirrel away a sum of money for their golden years without losing the bulk of it to the taxman. I may be totally off the mark here, but I'll bet that those goals are similar to what you want to do with your own money. You are not a bad person for wanting those things or for trying to earn that money through employment, and those who try to earn that money through business are not bad people either.

Nor is it the case that corporate entities wanting to make a profit are run by bad people. True, directors are accountable to their shareholders, but shareholders are not bad people, either. Shareholders are people just like you and me who have chosen to invest some of their savings in the riskier world of corporate equities rather than in the safer world of interest-earning bank accounts. These people are taking a risk in the hopes of reaping higher rewards, but that doesn't make them bad people.

We might not like the way some corporations distribute their money, with disproportionally large salaries at the top and low salaries at the bottom, but that situation doesn't make profit bad in itself. Many companies find ways to distribute profit to their employees very fairly.

The notion that wealth is evil gets a lot of play in popular culture. Movie villains are often wealthy, playing on a popular sentiment that wealth is a result of greed and selfishness. But it's greed and selfishness that are the evils, not wealth itself. Merely wanting to make a profit is not a bad goal.

What is evil is wanting to make a profit by defrauding people or taking advantage of their weaknesses. Those people who operate that way are scam artists and con men, preying on the innocent and gullible. We can all agree that those are nasty people. Let's all concede now that there's a special hell where those people will burn, and enough said about them. Rogues and charlatans are the exception, not the rule.

The bottom line: working at a for-profit corporation is not selling out to a less noble type of work.

Myth #2: Consultants are second-class workers

In the 20 years I worked as an independent consultant, I couldn't understood why it was so difficult to get a consulting gig with the government...but once I joined the civil service it was clear: too many people there see consultants as the "Enemy." They see consultants as overpriced professionals who don't understand the government's business, and who are out only to make a fast buck from its coffers.

Well, of course, some consultants are like that, but most aren't. Most consultants are people like you and me, who—for one reason or another—are not working for a single employer. The reasons vary immensely: some of them thrive on the variation of projects every few months. Some of them have tried to get a government job and can't. Some of them have unique skills that don't fit into full-time positions, that are required by a variety of organizations in small doses, and so on.

I heard a lot of complaints over the years from my civil service colleagues that outside consultants don't understand how government works. I have two responses to those complaints.

First, to a certain degree you may be correct. By not being in the position that you are, the outside consultant doesn't have the knowledge of the inner workings that you do. A good consultant will know where their knowledge falls short. But the converse of that disadvantage is that having worked with a variety of organizations, the consultant has more breadth of experience than you do. It is the combination of their breadth of experience with your knowledge of the inner workings of government that produces the best results.

Secondly, were you to leave your public service position and become a consultant, you would not suffer from that shortcoming. Your years working in government would give you some insight that people who've never worked in government do not have. If you can gain some breadth of experience and combine it with that insight, you would be a desirable commodity indeed!

There are many advantages to consulting, and there's no reason why being a consultant can't be a rewarding career for you if you have that inclination.

Myth #3: Job security lies in the demand for the activity you do rather than for the skills you have.

This myth is a variety of what I call the "preaching problem." The preaching problem is what happens when the church closes down and the reverend decides to change careers. At every interview he goes to they ask him what his skills are. If his answer is, "I'm great at preaching," then only religious organizations will hire him. On the other hand, if he says, "I'm great at public speaking," then a whole world opens up for him.

Public servants tend to make the same mistake. Take Céline, for example, an individual whose job it is to review applications for subsidies for corn farmers. Céline feels secure in her job only so long as the corn farmer subsidy program continues to exist. Even the suggestion that the government might be cutting that program is enough to push her to panic mode.

The problem is that fundamentally, Céline doesn't see herself as a knowledge worker, an information analyst, or a decision-maker. She doesn't see herself as a collection of skills and competencies; rather, she sees herself as a worker on the assembly line of that particular model subsidy application. She believes the myth. As a result, she is afraid that if they stop producing that model, she will lose her job.

Part of her fear is justified because of the way the government handles downsizing. This topic will be discussed more fully later on in this book, but for now

In the Real World, job security is based on the demand for your skills suffice it to say that when the government needs to cut down the number of subsidy application reviewers from eight to four, they're not going to choose which individuals to let go based on the quality of their work.

In the Real World, employers want to keep the best employees, so Céline's job depends on her being good at what she does. Her job security rests on the demand for her skills.

In the public service, it is not acceptable to conclude that some employees are better than others. As a result, people who make job cuts must resort to other criteria, and the criteria they choose may not be to Céline's advantage.

Myth #4: Full-time work is 40 hours per week

This myth pervades many industries.

✧ Margot ✧

Margot Yeates (not her real name) had been employed in the school system for 30 years. She had started there as an English teacher, and worked all the way up to the position of school principal, which she held for the last ten years. She was doing well financially, and her partner was bringing in enough income that she really didn't have to work for a living anymore. It was time for a change. So Margot found a 25-hour-a-week position helping out at a local old age home. She loved it, and it was giving her a lot of satisfaction to be working with older people and giving back to the community.

"I think I need to find some other work to supplement my job," she confided in me one day. "It's not that I need the money," she conceded, "It's just that I feel guilty not working full time."

Who determined that working 25 hours per week is not working full time? The tax department? The labour code? The unemployment insurance people? Talk about an historical vestige still hanging around in our society!

That notion was born in the days when employers abused employees by having them work 12 hours a day, seven days a week. Since that time, workers' rights legislation has gradually been reducing the number of hours per week that an employer is allowed to consider regular time. When an employee works above that number of hours the employer is required to pay an overtime wage.

Forty hours a week might be an appropriate test when it comes to determining whether an employee is being abused at the hand of the employer, but it is totally irrelevant when it comes to determining the number of hours you need to be working before **you** consider it full time.

No one has put this argument forward more eloquently than Tim Ferriss in his best-selling book *The 4-Hour Work Week*.[5] Don't get fooled by the title; it's not that everyone's goal should be a four-hour work week. In his book, Ferriss details the history of how we have come to believe that we need a certain minimum hours of work each week in order to feel that we're carrying our weight in the world.

But that's a myth, clear and simple. You should work as many hours as you want to work. If you're happy working 30 hours a week, and that brings you enough reward— financial and otherwise—that is full-time enough.

Towards the end of my time working in the government, I reduced my work week to a four-day work week, at 80% of the salary, and stayed at that level for a year and a half. Then I reduced it to a three-day work week at 60% of the salary.

Absolutely no amount of money could make up for the improvement in the quality of life I experienced by having

---

[5] Tim Ferriss: *The 4-Hour Work Week: Escape 9–5, Live Anywhere, and Join the New Rich*

the flexibility on those other days to do what I really wanted to do.

Myth #5: Work is never going to be fun

"If it were fun," my parents used to tell me, "then it wouldn't be called 'work.' Everyone would want to do it, and you wouldn't get paid for it."

It's easy to see where this myth comes from. Many people's work is really no fun at all. Very few people think that construction work is fun, or twisting widgets on an assembly line is fun, or tilling the field is fun. Manual labour is called "labour" for a reason.

But don't let that obscure the fact that for many people work actually is fun. They love what they do. They work to make a difference in the lives of others every day. People pursuing their dreams, where their work is part of their dreams.

Working in the health and wellness fields, or with children, or animals, or other care-taking fields easily provides ample opportunities to improve other people's lives.

Obviously, not everyone who works in those fields is deliriously happy; there are many people who do not enjoy working in those occupations. But those who do enjoy it find their work extremely rewarding.

The key is to find out what is rewarding for you.

Links to sources and other
resources are available on the
Unlocking the Golden Handcuffs web site
www.goldenhandcuffs.net/

The Businessman and the Fisherman
A CAREER PARABLE

A wealthy businessman took a trip to the Caribbean, to spend a week relaxing away from his enormously stressful business. He decided to go fishing, and found someone who took tourists out in his small boat on day trips.

The outing was a great success: half a dozen good-size fish, beautiful weather, fresh air...the businessman noted how relaxed he felt floating on the water under the bright sun. He was particularly impressed with his guide, a 30-year-old local man who was able to navigate the waters very well. The local was relaxed, healthy looking, and seemed very content doing what he was doing.

Towards the end of the day the businessman struck up a conversation. He learned that the local had been doing the same work for ten years, and that he liked it a lot. He got to meet new people, spend his days out on the water, and working six days a week he managed to earn a good living.

"And what do you do in the evenings?" asked the businessman.

"After work, I go to the gym," he said. "Then my wife and I go for a quiet dinner with some friends, and

The Businessman and the Fisherman

afterwards we all sit around a campfire on the beach drinking wine and chatting."

The businessman was struck by this man's lack of ambition for something greater. He saw an opportunity to show the local a better way.

"You know," he ventured cautiously, "you could turn this into a real successful business if you wanted to."

"What do you mean?" the local asked.

"Well, you're doing this all by yourself." The business-man prepared himself to teach the local a set of new concepts. "If you had people doing this work for you, you could pay them a salary and make a good profit on the side."

The local was definitely in new territory. "Why would I want to do that?" he asked.

"That way you wouldn't have a mere job, but you would be running your own business."

"Okay," the local responded, genuinely intrigued. "And why is that better?"

"You can't grow your job," explained the businessman. "But your business can grow in size."

"And why would I want it to grow in size?"

The Businessman and the Fisherman

The businessman continued, "The more people you have working for you, the more money you can make. Eventually you could have a fleet of boats and a full staff of people."

"And then?"

"Don't you see?" The businessman was growing a bit frustrated. "Then you can continue to build it up, so you're heading up a national corporation, and eventually an international corporation. You could be employing hundreds or thousands of people, and making millions of dollars."

The local seemed to have lost interest. "Tell me," he asked. "Why I would want to be making millions of dollars?"

"I can't believe you're asking that question!" the businessman said. "If you had millions of dollars you'd be rich! You could take a vacation whenever you wanted! Can't you see that?" The businessman then softened his tone.

"Wouldn't you like to be able to do what I do, to come down to these beautiful waters and go fishing every day? To relax at the end of every day and spend the evening drinking wine with your friends?"

The local looked him straight in the eye. He shrugged his shoulders. "I do that now," he said quietly.

Chapter 4

THE PUBLIC SERVICE IS NOT THE REAL WORLD

I'll repeat that: the public service is not the Real World.

If you've worked only in the public service your whole life, you may wonder why anyone would say that. After all, your job seems just as real as everyone else's job.

You come to work in the morning and leave at the end of the day. You have a supervisor you report to and perhaps you also have subordinates who report to you. You have tasks to be done, deadlines to meet, and calls to return. You attend too many meetings, follow office procedures when ordering pens, submit absence reports for sick days, and there's always another form to fill out. It sure seems like a real job.

You're right, the public service job is real. The people are real and the pay is real. The pressure is real and the aggravation is real.

What's not real is the environment. Government is a universe unto itself. If you look at it solely from the inside, that's not readily apparent. You can see how it differs from other environments only when you compare them side by side.

1. Income vs. Expense

In the Real World—that is, everywhere outside government—real forces are at work. The course of events is dictated by market forces like supply and demand, and by bleak financial realities, such as the fact that business can't levy taxes the way government does.

Every activity in a Real World organization either brings in money or spends money. In the Real World, the financial consequences of an action are paramount. People who make decisions do so while considering the cost implications of each alternative, and everyone understands that time wasted is money wasted.

While the Government brings in money through taxes, fees, and other duties, those incoming funds are not tied directly to people's time. We don't bring in more taxes by working longer hours. Moreover, the government will continue to collect taxes independently of the activities of any individual department. Most public servants, therefore, are never required to think in terms of income versus expenditure.

This difference has enormous implications. In the Real World, even a decision as simple as whether or not to hold a meeting is made in full recognition that having people sit in a room carrying on a conversation has a calculable cost.

Government doesn't look at expenditures the same way. Its meetings are convened as if they don't cost a cent. When you think meetings are free, there's no reason not to have more of them!

2. Long Term Planning

As a democratic nation, we are fortunate enough to have an elected government. When the people want the ruling party to take a different direction, they have the opportunity and the tools to oust it and replace it with one that promises something better. This ability to hold the government responsive to the electorate is a pillar of our democracy. Through that mechanism, we are spared the long-term dictatorships that oppress some other, less fortunate nations.

The turnover of elected officials, however, makes long-term planning more difficult.

No government can legally bind its successors. The implications of that fact are that governments often don't worry about long-term consequences; they will be someone else's problem. The vast majority of plans made are short term or, at best, medium term.

Short-term plans are too often just quick fixes. Without the requirement to plan long-term, quick fixes get bandaged over again and again. The incentive to rebuild infrastructure properly is not consistent with short-term planning. Moreover, many projects stay in "pilot mode" for years, because a pilot or test period is a short-term commitment, even when it is perpetually renewed.

In the Real World, the longevity of ownership and account-ability deters short-sighted solutions. People have much more freedom to plan for the long term. The same people who make the decision today will be living with it in ten or twenty years, so it might as well be done right the first time.

3. Limited Priorities

In the Real World, priorities are things that need to be taken care of first. Since there is a cost both to delaying a priority and to carrying out a priority, senior management weighs the costs of carrying out the priority against the return it will bring. At the end of the day, some individual at the top will make a decision as to which priorities are most important. At that point, management will distribute the list of two or three top priorities, and everyone will concentrate on those. The rest will be declared "not a priority."

Those of you who have never worked in government might be wondering how that could be any different in the civil service. Surely, the government has priorities, doesn't it?

Yes, of course it does. Many. Hundreds of them, in fact. All top priority.

In one government office I worked in, some two dozen managers spent a full day trying to narrow down our activities to determine what our priority projects were going to be for the coming year—in addition to our ongoing work, **all of which** was considered a priority. The result at the end of the day was a list of no less than **72 priority projects**, none of which was actually independently funded. Senior management was willing to concede that we couldn't possibly give priority to six dozen different projects at the same time, so we were told instead that the first half of the list would be given priority in the current quarter, and we would be expected to concentrate on the second half of the list after that.

In the Real World, were an organization to decide that it was going to concentrate on 36 priorities over a three-month period, it would resource those priorities with money, people, and time, being the three standard elements of project management. No one would expect 36 priorities all to be front and centre at the same time, all drawing from a single bucket of funds.

4. Emergencies

In the Real World, an emergency is when someone is in danger of losing their health or life. When people are bleeding on the side of the road after a car accident, that's an emergency.

Some areas of government deal in real emergencies, for example, the military, the police, public safety services, and so on. These organizations have very tough jobs to do, and they use the term *emergency* properly.

Outside of these organizations, too many government officials have lost perspective.

I'm sure I wasn't the only public servant who worked in an office where an emergency would be declared when a spelling mistake was found in a document on the government web site. In that office, everything else had to come to a halt so we could direct our efforts to preventing this typographic crisis. And we're not talking about a significant word here; we're talking about a typo in the middle of a sentence in an economic report. Some poor proofreader obviously missed fixing that one, and an emergency was declared.

In the government, emergencies are declared because a presentation deck is going up to a senior manager's office and one slide is incomplete. Emergencies are declared because someone decided to leave on holiday a day early and bring a deadline forward 24 hours. Emergencies are declared because somebody wants something *Now!* and doesn't care how much work it takes to get it.

To those who risk their lives daily putting out fires, extracting injured passengers from crushed vehicles, or containing some kid high on cocaine and brandishing a loaded weapon, using the word *emergency* to describe a spelling mistake in a document is a joke. It's an insult to the good work of real emergency workers.

In the Real World emergencies are not declared lightly. Sending in resources to perform work without immediate regard to the cost is something we do to save lives, not bad spelling. If someone were to declare an emergency based on a typo, they would do so knowing the cost of shutting down other services to fix the problem.

5. Expectations Proportionate to Funding

The main goal of business is to make a profit. The main goal of government is to deliver a service. Everybody knows that, but not everybody understands the implications of that difference, more specifically, how that difference manifests itself when setting expectations around projects. In the Real World they adjust their expectations to the level of funding; whereas, in the government they don't seem to do that.

✧ Carla ✧

Carla Malczeki (not her real name) was a business analyst and IT specialist who was looking at taking a consulting position with one of the provincial governments. The department administering business incorporation wanted to build a new system that enabled individuals to do online corporate registration, reducing the need for counter services.

Carla arrived in the senior manager's office, and was seated so they could explain the project to her.

"We want to build a world-class, leading-edge, online corporate registration system," the manager explained grandly. "It should be top-notch, innovative, and help showcase our talents to other governments in the country and the world."

Carla was intrigued. "And what's the budget for this system?" she asked. Carla had worked on several multi-million dollar projects and understood the extent of the costs involved.

The manager responded definitively, "$250,000."

Carla's mouth fell open. Even in those days that amount was a paltry sum for a project of this scale.

"Okay," she proceeded cautiously. "What you're going to end up with is not a world-class, leading-edge system, but the best system you can buy for $250,000." Considering that government projects are funded from the public purse, building a good, functional system— rather than a world-class one—would not have been an unreasonable goal.

The manager, however, did not think that the proposed budget might be insufficient.

"No," he insisted. "We want to build the best system available in the world today."

The conversation began to deteriorate, and shortly thereafter Carla left the building. Need I add that she didn't take the job?

Businesses in the Real World approach these matters differently. They know that at the end of the day they must produce a deliverable that is demonstrably of greater value than the amount spent. They would have started by calculating the financial value of a having a world-class, leading-edge system, and only then determining the maximum amount of money they could spend on it before it became a liability rather than an asset.

If we don't calculate the value of the final product first, then we have no baseline to work against. In that case, the only basis upon which to decide how much money to spend is what's in our pockets. The government, not being concerned with profit, often doesn't do that calculation. The goal is to offer the best service, and it costs whatever it costs. It's a tough challenge.

Government will persist whether or not it makes realistic promises; whereas, organizations in the Real World have to be more careful. They don't pledge achievable goals to their customers in order to get re-elected, they do it to stay alive. A consumer goods company that doesn't meet its promises feels the backlash in a very financial way, and if the company is to survive it needs to be realistic about what it can promise. The principle that one doesn't promise what one can't produce makes its way down to every level of a Real World organization. Anyone working in that environment needs to remain acutely aware of that principle.

6. Incentive to Produce More

In rare cases, revenue generated by a government program directly offsets the costs of that program; e.g., the fees collected from the issuance of drivers' licences may be used to offset the costs of running the licensing program. In this case, the more efficiently licences can be issued, the more revenue can be generated.

In most cases, however, the link is not direct. The fines collected from the prosecution of traffic offences do not make their way to the government offices involved in that enforcement: the police, the judiciary, the court administration, and so on. Convicting more people of speeding doesn't produce income as a reward, since the costs of a given prosecution significantly outweigh the fine. Similarly, any fees charged for the production of documents under Freedom of Information (Access to Information) legislation are not redirected to the work areas that assemble and release those documents. In short, the level at which people work is unrelated to their compensation.

In contrast, in the Real World higher production often means higher revenues. There's a financial incentive to work harder, and people who work hard can reap the benefits.

7. Staffing

Hold onto your seats, fellow Public Servants, because this section is going to blow you away!

Do you know how long a job hiring process takes in the Real World? Not the nine to twelve months it takes it in the longest cases in the public service. Not even the three or four months it takes in most public service jobs.

Whereas a public service job competition can be "rushed" so that as few as eight weeks pass between job posting and the letter of offer, even that length of time is considered overly protracted in the private sector. Expect your job application process to take between three and six weeks. In fact, a private sector organization has the ability to hire someone within one week, or even one day, if it wants to.

The implications of that are enormous. Positions are not held vacant for months on end while a staffing process takes place. Temporary help can be hired very quickly to bridge the gap during the staffing process to help with the workload.

The private sector does not put up with the nonsense that is commonplace in the public sector, where positions stay empty for months or years, while hiring is slowed down by unnecessarily rigid and complex staffing processes, even though hundreds of clearly qualified candidates are ready, willing, and able to take the job and start working.

Incidentally, the private sector knows that staffing your position includes staffing it during your vacation. Unlike the public service, where you can return to the office only to find unexpectedly that your work was left to languish for three weeks while you were gone, in the private sector someone may actually plan to cover you in your absence.

In the Real World we are unlikely to see the common government practice where someone's absence is "covered" by no more than a peremptory out-of-office message advising of their return date. That lack of customer service is unacceptable in the Real World, because an out-of-office message can cause a potential customer to turn away and search for a competitor.

8. Project Management

In the last few years, government has become a lot better at managing both large and small scale ventures as projects, following generally accepted project management principles. Unfortunately, there are still too many exceptions.

That organization I told you about earlier—the one that narrowed down its business plans to 72 priorities—decided to bring in a project consultant to plan how to manage them all. Senior management had set the scene for the consultant ahead of time, explaining that we had some 50 projects that were ongoing or in development. From that introduction, the consultant was initially led to believe that lots was happening.

But the consultant was from the Real World, and for each project he asked the same set of questions:

"You say that this project is in progress. Have resources been committed to it?"

"No, not yet," was the answer.

"Then have resource requirements been determined?"

"No, not yet."

"Have the milestones been identified?"

"No."

"Has a timeline been set?"

"Nope."

"Is there a budget?"

"Um, not really."

"Is there a project Charter, at least?"

"No, no charter yet."

"Then why do you consider this project in progress?"

As you can imagine, the consultant asked this last question with a little bit of exasperation.

The responses to this question varied depending on the project:

"…because we've had several discussions about it."

"…because we're working on it with another group."

"…because it's been on the table for a while."

"…because it's a commitment that was made by a senior official."

"… because it's been announced to the public."

The consultant replied with what people in the Real World know instinctively:

"No charter, no budget, no resources?" he said. "That's called 'Concept Stage.'"

Of over 50 "projects" discussed that day, it turned out that three quarters of them were actually still the in concept stage.

In the Real World, practicality is the rule. A project is not described as "in progress" until it is scoped, funded, and resourced.

9. Results over Process

Government is process driven. In the Real World, they value results over process. Fortunately, the Real World isn't hamstrung by process checks and balances that have stretched what are fundamentally good principles to idiotic levels through blind application in all circumstances. Permit me to illustrate the difference with this story about my attempt to hire temporary help while in the government.

A few years back I was acting as Director of Corporate Integrated Records Services for a large government department. Included in that portfolio was the responsibility for all the centrally run records rooms housing the paper files of the organization.

One day, we received ridiculously late notice of an impending move. We were vacating a storey in one of the buildings we occupied, and several thousands of file folders needed to be boxed and moved before the end of the week.

An urgent need for non-permanent, minimally skilled work is exactly the right kind of situation to reach for temporary help services. It ensures that the regular employees are not pulled off their work to deal with the distraction, doesn't jeopardize anybody's job, and is reasonably cost-efficient under the circumstances.

When we first learned about the situation, we had only a general sense about the volume of files from the number of file cabinets. I kickstarted the process for hiring temporary employees by putting in a request for two employees. Several companies were approached with a general statement of qualifications and asked to propose candidates. From these, we would select two individuals to help us out. The process from top to bottom takes a few days, and so I didn't expect the employees to be able to start work until the end of the week. Not optimal, but workable. While we waited for the temporary help to arrive, one of our permanent people went over to try to make a dent in the situation.

After a couple of days working on the project, our employees were able to give us a better sense of the situation we were facing. It turned out that the volume of files was greater than had been estimated initially. Moreover, many of the files carried a security categorization of "Secret," and those required special handling. The prudent thing to do, to ensure that the job would be complete by the deadline, would be to increase the number of temporary help workers assigned to the job. As it was, the process was taking longer than it should have, leaving us behind schedule. I sent a note asking that the number of temporary helpers be increased from two to three.

Silly me. Adjusting the number of employees requested after the process has been started is not permitted, because it is considered an abuse of process. The process must be completely restarted, this time specifying three employees. Changing that number midstream apparently jeopardizes the integrity of equitable treatment for temporary help agencies around the entire country, if not the globe.

"We sent your request to companies that indicated they would be willing to provide two employees," I was told. "It wouldn't be fair to everyone else if we changed that request and asked for three employees. It is possible that some companies that said no to our request for two wouldn't have said no had they known we might really want three, and we have unfairly excluded those companies." (I know this logic is hard to follow, but try to be understanding; these people are just following the process.)

Time was running out and I was getting desperate. Maybe we could just start a new process for the third employee? You know, request a single employee that we could add to the other two.

Nope. Not possible. Breaking down larger contracts into smaller ones for practical purposes is completely *verboten*. The practice is called "contract splitting," and will raise the eyebrows of anybody who gets wind of it.

The reason for prohibiting contract splitting is very valid. It's to ensure that people don't take large value contracts—which by necessity have many conditions that they need to comply with—and split them into small value contracts simply to avoid the conditions. That's completely understandable. If contracts over a certain amount, e.g., $100,000, need to go for review before a certain committee, then splitting them into small contracts to avoid that review is clearly an attempt to skirt the rules.

A Real World organization would maintain perspective in these kinds of situations. Someone would look at my request for an additional employee for the week, and examine the circumstances. Within 30 seconds, they would come to the realization that I was not attempting to skirt the rules, but that in a time-sensitive situation the contract requests had simply unfolded in a certain manner. No Real World employer would insist in this circumstance that we cancel the first request for two employees and start fresh.

Real World employers are much more likely to handle these types of situations practically. With the focus on results and not process, working in the Real World gives you access to a wider variety of solutions in situations when you need to handle difficult logistics.

10. Timelines and Deadlines

In the Real World, committing to a timeline means something. In the manufacturing, retail, and commercial industries, delay has a direct impact on sales, which has an impact on revenues, and therefore profits. Organizations can seldom afford to be late to market; tardiness has cost some companies their very existence.

Not getting a product out to market on schedule can mean losing market share or a competitive advantage to someone who was quicker. When that loss is significant, everyone up and down the line feels the repercussions: salaries don't go up, bonuses can't be paid, shareholders don't receive big dividends, and so on. If the product isn't ready to go when it is supposed to be ready to go, heads would start to roll, figuratively speaking. Most likely somebody would be fired if timelines are continually not met.

Government is different. Being a monopoly has its advantages. When one has no competitors, timelines don't mean anything. If a program was supposed to begin on January 1st and it's late, the only people who suffer are the targeted beneficiaries of the program.

The absence of a cascading-down effect means that government lacks one of the incentives that private business has for meeting timelines.

✦ Kyle ✦

Kyle Bolduc (not his real name) is an application infrastructure analyst. He worked for five years with the federal government before he gave it up for a job in the private sector. He left feeling frustrated and discouraged.

"Things go much faster now," he says. "Timelines in the government are ridiculous. The application I worked on took over a year to roll out, and that's after almost a whole year of requirements gathering. In my new company the entire project would probably take just a few months. Within a year we'd be able to see the results of implementation and feel like we made a difference."

Kyle vividly remembers the project delays. He fully expected at the time that someone in the higher ranks might be unhappy that the process took so long. No such luck; on the contrary, they seemed pleased about how well they had run that project.

"We even got an award for it!" he says flabbergasted. "It was the biggest train wreck I have ever worked on my whole career, and they gave us an award as if it were a job well done."

Kyle is much more satisfied working in the private sector, where the people at the top can tell the difference between a successful deployment of an application and a train wreck, and don't reward the latter.

Now I'm not suggesting that the Real World is never late in its product delivery. Anyone who's ever bought a new home with the promise that it would be built and ready by a certain date has experienced buyers' angst as the deadline gets closer.

Sometimes the deadline gets pushed back several times. If the contract is structured in the buyer's favour, there may be a penalty to the seller for being late, such as a rebate in price of some kind or an optional feature added to the deal. Whatever it is, at some point the penalty will have an impact on the bottom line. True, the reputation of the builder may also be at stake, but usually where the consequences are financial they are more concerned about those consequences than about the damage to their reputation.

In the government, there are rarely financial consequences to not meeting a deadline. Failing to set up a program on time, not purchasing a product on time, whatever it is, there are no penalties. The key dates on a project timetable roll over more than logs rushing down the Fraser river.

If you are someone who likes planning timelines and then sticking to them, you might find more satisfaction from the respect a timeline is given in the Real World.

The working world outside of government is often called "private industry," mostly because for-profit corporations offer the majority of jobs in this sector. But don't limit yourself if you don't have to. Other types of organizations can also be good workplaces, such as charitable, educational, research and other non-profit associations, cooperative ventures, and international organizations. Some of these workplaces suffer from some of the ills listed in this chapter, but only government combines them all.

Chapter 5

Desirable Job Skills in the Real World

If you make yourself indispensable to your employer, he is not going to part with you in a hurry no matter what it costs him.

~ Robert Baden-Powell

As a public servant reading Lord Baden-Powell's statement, you might wonder what world he lived in. This sure doesn't describe any reality that you know.

His statement is actually true in the Real World. In the Real World people don't give away things of value. They keep them, they sell them, or they trade them, but it's always based on the recognition that good help is hard to find, and value is related to supply and demand.

In the Real World, the more talent you have and the rarer the talent, the more value you have. The best lawyers charge more money than the average ones, the best salespeople earn more commissions than the average ones, and the best chocolate cakes command better prices than the average ones.

It's unfortunate that Lord Baden-Powell's statement is not applicable in the public service. The disregard for the value of certain talents—especially rare or unique ones—is frustrating for the people who have them.

Some job competencies are in common supply in the government. Large numbers of people have very good analytical thinking skills, data analysis skills, program planning skills, and accounting skills. On the other hand, you'll find far fewer individuals who really excel at idea generation, creativity, collaboration, change management, networking, and so on.

This lopsided distribution is not haphazard. In the Real World, results are more important than process. The skills required in the Real World are therefore more results oriented than process driven.

One of the saddest things I witnessed when I worked in the public service was how it quickly it extinguishes the sparks of creativity that individuals bring to the table. Its deep-seated culture of risk aversion, inertia, and distrust of change makes innovation an uphill battle, despite the lip service that's paid to it.

I worked at one point on a business improvement team, whose job it was to find inefficiencies and problems inside processes and recommend improvements to them. It was a formidable challenge. It seemed that people were happy to improve their processes, so long as they didn't have to change anything! Innovation was good but change was bad. Creativity was treated as individualistic non-conformity. "That's not the way we do it" was the most common sentence I heard that year.

✧ Trevor ✧

Trevor Banks has been a public servant for over 20 years. He is clever, quirky, innovative, and a risk-taker. He's not afraid to shake the trees to see what falls down. Yet the public service in no way takes advantage of his unique talents.

"In rare instances," he confides, "under the right manager, I have had glimpses of success. Mostly, though, innovation is shoved through a filtration system of approvals, and spat out in the same tired, old, cookie-cutter format."

> The skills required in Real World are more results oriented than process driven

"Even when it comes to the need to generate enthusiasm or support for a new initiative, when you'd think that unusual or eye-catching approaches would be welcomed, it's not the case."

I've seen Trevor in action. As a presenter, he has real people skills. He knows how to connect with an audience to create trust. He can read the energy in a room and make extemporaneous adjustments to his presentation, ensuring that the audience stays attentive until the very end.

There's no place for people like Trevor in the public service. He resisted accepting that fact for a long time and now concedes that he can't change the system. Still, he hasn't given up hope.

"Since creativity is the essence of effective promotion and marketing, I'm going to keep shopping my skills around until I find the right home for them."

I agree with him; shopping his skills around is what he should be doing. He will be right at home when he can find work in areas like business improvement, change management, organizational culture, transformation of roles, and similar people-centric initiatives within a larger project or program.

But that home is unlikely to be in the public service. According to one report on the notorious failed implementation of the Phoenix pay system, those areas are exactly the components of the project that were totally neglected.[6] They either appeared only peripherally in early project documentation or were ignored completely.

And that pattern repeats itself in government projects all too often.

✧ Derek ✧

Derek Burrows, a project manager at IBM, remembers his early days working for a regional government.

"Originality is not a particularly desirable trait for an employee to have, especially a junior employee," Derek asserts. "The government doesn't hire people because of their ability to do independent thinking." He is very happy to have left the public service. Eventually, he ended up working at IBM.

"It's much different in the private sector," Derek explains. "As an example, one of the corporate values they promote at IBM is "Treasure wild ducks." Uniqueness and

---

[6] Treasury Board of Canada Secretariat: Lessons Learned from the Transformation of Pay Administration Initiative
https://www.canada.ca/en/treasury-board-secretariat/corporate/reports/lessons-learned-transformation-pay-administration-initiative.html

distinctiveness bring a competitive advantage to the organization, and management here welcomes people who think differently."

Derek gets to use his creativity and his resourcefulness in his work.

"The difference in attitude is remarkable," he says. "I know that my unique combination of skills and talents allows me to bring a certain approach to each project, and management assigns me to specific projects that can benefit from it."

Are you a creative individual? Do you love coming up with innovative solutions to problems? Does the work you produce have an originality to it that only you can bring? Do you value your uniqueness?

There are companies out in the Real World that are looking for people exactly like you. They want somebody different, not somebody the same. They want somebody excellent, not somebody average.

> # Uniqueness and distinctiveness are a competitive advantage

Are you an idea factory? Coming up with new ideas all the time about different approaches to try and different ways to do things? There are lots places where that skill is extraordinarily valuable. If you find one that really appreciates what you have to offer, you will love your work.

Links to sources and other
resources are available on the
Unlocking the Golden Handcuffs web site
www.goldenhandcuffs.net/

Chapter 6

JOB INTERVIEWS IN THE REAL WORLD

In the Real World a job interview is an opportunity for the employer to get to know you and for you to get to know them. What a concept! Unlike the public service, where the job interview is basically an oral examination, the private sector uses the interview to have an honest-to-goodness discussion.

The way interviewers pose questions in public service interviews—reading them *verbatim* from a script, then staring at you blankly while scribbling notes, being careful not to indicate on their faces whether or not you have the right answer—is not useful in the Real World.

A Real World interview is a two-way process. The interviewer will listen intently to what you have to say and interact with you. Just like a normal human discussion— the same way people have conversations everyday. Who'd have thought it possible?

Public Service Job Competitions

For those of you who have never been through a public service job competition, the above paragraphs about interviews may seem a tad ridiculous. Let me take a moment to explain how job competitions work in the civil service. The rules surrounding hiring are strict and complex, and breaking even one rule is grounds for a lawsuit or a grievance at the hands of the aggrieved candidate.

Jobs in the civil service are "posted," meaning that they are advertised to a defined group of people for a defined period.

When a job is posted, a site is set up somewhere where candidates can go for an explanation of each of the job qualifications, specifically, the skills, the knowledge, and the behavioural competencies sought.

A behavioural competency would be something like "judgment" or "decisiveness."

The inclusion of a skill, knowledge area or competency in the qualifications is a strong indication that candidates are going to be tested on them, either prior to or during the interview. "Tested?" you ask. It's easy to test knowledge, and relatively easy to test some skills like writing, research, and presentation skills, but how does one test for competencies like judgment and decisiveness in an interview?

Of course, they can't actually test for behavioural competencies like judgment and decisiveness unless they put the candidate into a situation where the candidate has to use judgment or decisiveness. That would have to be a very sophisticated test indeed, and in the competitions for high ranking positions, it's not uncommon to undergo an elaborate, expertly-designed scenario simulation to provide that scoring.

Scenario simulation testing is expensive, so the civil service job interview has developed an alternative. In the interview, someone asks you to demonstrate the behavioural competency in question through an anecdote, e.g., "Tell us about a time at work when you were decisive." The candidate then has to tell the right story.

In typical bureaucratic fashion, the acceptable answers to this question have been established by a committee. A list of the attributes of each behavioural competency is posted online, and candidates are expected to review that list before coming to the interview.

For example, the indicators of a behavioural competency like decisiveness might be as follows:[7]

---

[7] Taken from a real government Web site

+ Selects solutions based on pre-identified alternatives or known options

+ Weighs appropriately available information when choosing the best protocol

+ Makes the right call; stays true and is not influenced by undue interferences or threats

It is insufficient that the candidate's answer demonstrates making a decision if the candidate cannot also demonstrate an understanding of what decisiveness is all about. For that reason, the prepared candidate will have memorized the wording of the attributes of the competency, and can regurgitate it in their story, lest someone think that the candidate merely makes decisions by accident.

A well-prepared candidate comes to the interview armed with the right anecdote. And what if a candidate doesn't actually have a suitable anecdote to tell? That's an easy problem to get around: the candidate can substitute a story about what the candidate **might have done** had the appropriate opportunity arisen. So long as the candidate regurgitates all the correct attributes, the interviewer will say that the candidate demonstrates an understanding of the behavioural competency. From there, the interviewer must conclude that they will be able to apply those attributes in the right circumstance. The answer to that question gets a checkmark. Next.

It would be interesting to know whether there is any independent evidence that this approach produces better qualified candidates. Do people who score well on questions around a particular competency actually demonstrate those attributes once they are working in the new job? Frankly, it would be much less work—and I suspect more reliable—simply to ask the candidate outright, "Are you a decisive individual?" and to accept the answer given.

Posted Job Qualifications

In the Real World, a job application is a completely different experience.

No list of attributes for the various competencies that they are looking for is available for checking online. You may even find that the competencies are not listed in the job posting. In fact, it might be only during the job interview that someone casually mentions that they're looking for an individual with "good people skills."

In a public service competition, that particular qualification had better be listed in the job posting. Expecting a candidate to have a skill that wasn't explicitly named in the job posting is an egregious error in the government hiring process. An omission of that nature is grounds for scrapping the entire competition and starting again!

The logic used to justify this approach is draconian. By omitting "good people skills" from the list of qualifications sought—according to the argument put forward—the list of candidates might contain some individuals who do not have people skills. Springing this terribly unusual job requirement upon those candidates amounts to an unfair labour practice or something equally sinister.

Even worse—the argument continues—there may be individuals looking for positions requiring good people skills who did not apply for that position, precisely because that qualification did not appear in the job posting. The introduction of that requirement at this point is considered terribly unfair to all the candidates looking for jobs requiring people skills. The process must now be restarted, with the newly required qualification included.

The Real World, in contrast, does not let jobs rise or fall on such technicalities. Do not be surprised if you go to an interview and find out that they are looking for something that did not appear in the job advertisement. In the Real World, employers are looking to hire people with the right fit. There are far too many components— both overt and subtle—to what makes the right fit to list in a job advertisement.

Get to Know One Another

Expect your job interview in the Real World to be an exploratory discussion for both you and the employer.

As you would when applying for a government job, you can learn about the employer's mission and goals on their Web site. Publicly traded companies also produce a *Report to Shareholders*, containing the information you'd find in a government department's *Report on Plans and Priorities*. Knowing the goals of the company helps you provide relevant and congruous answers to interview questions.

Moreover—and here's the kicker—you have the option of contacting the organization ahead of time to find out who the interviewer will be. You can then research that individual on a site like LinkedIn before going to meet them. By learning a little bit about them and their background, you can prepare yourself in advance to hit the right notes.

In a successful interview, you will end up having a very informative, respectful, **bi-directional** discussion. That's much more civilized than what passes for an interview in the public service.

Questions About Your Opinion

In a Real World job interview, the interviewer might throw in a question like, "What do you think of the new standard for soda pop bottles?" Questions eliciting your opinion on some relevant subject are not uncommon.

Answer those kinds of questions as honestly and articulately as you can. The truth is—and you might want to sit down for this one—that there are no pre-determined right or wrong answers to these questions!

That's right! The interviewer isn't asking you the question as a test to see if you have the right answer. **The interviewer actually wants to learn what you think**. The interviewer wants to know whether you have an opinion on something, whether you base your opinions on facts, whether you can reason them out, and how you express them. The interviewer might even challenge your response, to observe your reactions to a spontaneous exchange on the subject.

> Real World job interviews are a two-way conversation

There's no way for you to second guess the answer to this question. The interviewer might hate the new standard and be looking for an ally. The interviewer might love the new standard and be looking for support. The interviewer may not care a hoot about how you feel about the standard, so long as you can discuss it intelligently with other people.

The world is not black-and-white. In the Real World interview, questions are often an attempt to see how you handle various shades of grey. That approach sits in sharp contrast to the public service approach, where you would never be asked to discuss shades of grey—unless, of course, those shades of grey were defined in detail ahead of time and listed in an answer evaluation grid.

Some jobseekers are very uncomfortable with the loose structure of the Real World interview. They want to know that each question has a specific correct answer, and that those who get the correct answer, pass and those who don't, fail. If you are one of those who seeks mathematical certainty in the interview process, then you may be better suited to public-service-type interviews.

Do you have what it takes to do well at job interviews? Do you dress well, speak well, present well? Do you have a pleasant or friendly personality? In the Real World —in your work life just as in your social interaction—the way you dress, speak, and present yourself is meaningful.

None of those characteristics will do you any good at an interview for a government job unless the job posting specifically lists them as requirements. Realistically though, no public service job posting is going to list them that way, because that would entail coming up with standards for measuring how candidates do on that aspect of the interview.

When you go to a job interview in the Real world, let your personal attributes shine! Show the interviewer the kind of person you are, and let them want to hire you for being that person.

Links to sources and other
resources are available on the
Unlocking the Golden Handcuffs web site
www.goldenhandcuffs.net/

Chapter 7

CAREER ADVANCEMENT IN THE REAL WORLD

...lie down with dogs, and you wake up with a raise and a promotion.

Watch What Happens, *from* Newsies

With these lyrics, up-and-coming newspaper reporter Katherine Plumber informs us that if she does a good job covering the story of the newsboys' strike she will be rewarded accordingly.

Getting a raise or a promotion as a reward for a job well done may never happen in the public service, but it sure happens a lot in the Real World.

✧ Kyle ✧

In an earlier chapter I introduced Kyle, an application infrastructure analyst who left the government for the private sector. He had had a terrible time moving up the ladder in the government office. Not so in his new organization.

"Sometimes they run competitions," he explains, "but often they just promote people who do a good job into a higher position."

Does Kyle feel that this is somehow unfair? Does he feel that due process is not respected? Not at all.

In the public service, it is considered inequitable if every possible candidate is not given the opportunity to compete for every single position. In the Real World, things work differently, and often that difference works to your advantage.

"Personal accomplishment is recognized," he says. "If you can do a good job, you can get on management's radar, and they'll watch your performance over time. It doesn't take long before they reward it."

Even when jobs are offered through competition in the private sector, the interval between job posting and hiring can be as little as a few weeks. Although there are cases in the public service where—solely by the fortuitous coincidence of circumstances—someone moves up through the ranks in a relatively short period of time, those cases are the exception. Your career has the potential to advance much faster in the Real World than it can in the public service.

No Pegging At Level

Unlike the public service, private sector employers don't use a common set of job classifications. While universally standardized job classifications may have some advantages, they have drawbacks as well.

From a career advancement point of view, you are adversely affected if you are one of those who joined the civil service by accepting an entry level job below your skill levels, just to get a foot in the door. Once you've done that, you are notionally "pegged" at that lower classification, even if it doesn't truly represent your skills. If you originally accepted, for example, a Level 2 administrative position as a means to gain entry to the public service, from that point on you were pegged as a Level-2-administration-type individual, despite your actual skills and qualifications, and you likely found that trying to move up to positions more appropriate to your skill level was a struggle.

The people reviewing job candidates' resumés are subtly influenced by an applicant's current level. If it looks like a candidate is trying to advance too many steps at one time, the candidate is viewed as overly ambitious. Reviewers rarely entertain the possibility that the applicant originally accepted a job below their skill level.

In the Real World, no one knows what a government Level 2 administrative position means. Instead, they'll look at your qualifications without the taint of whatever level you were pegged at in the public service.

No Union Influence

Most of the Real World is free from one of the major impediments to career growth in the public service: the unions. One would be hard-pressed to find another white collar industry that embraces unions the way the public service does.

Unions have a lengthy history in government operations. The federal civil service in Canada more than doubled in size during the course of World War II, when new programs like Unemployment Insurance and Baby Bonus cheques required large numbers of people to support them.[8] Over the next decade or so they took a firm foothold, and by the end of the 1960s, most public sector employees across Canada had been unionized.[9]

Clearly, unions do provide a number of benefits to civil service employees, such as collective bargaining, a standardized grievance procedure, and representation

---

[8] A Coming of Age: Counselling Canadians for Work in the Twentieth Century

[9] *ibid.*

of the employee perspective in a variety of circumstances such as health and safety reviews and working conditions.

But there's also a cost. Today the unions are involved in far more aspects of employment than those listed above.

Unions are significant in this chapter because they contribute to making government job classifications so inflexible and moving up the ladder so difficult.

Jobs in the public service all have different levels, starting at Level 1 and increasing, each with more responsibility and coordinately higher salary. A Level 3 widget specialist is allowed to work at specific activities that have been deemed appropriate to that level.

If, for example, widget washing is classified as a Level 4 activity, then a Level 3 employee assigned widget washing duties must be paid a Level 4 salary. Conversely, assigning a Level 3 duty to a Level 4 employee is seen as taking work away from other Level 3 employees, so the practice is discouraged.

These types of rigid constraints are clearly the product of a previous era. They are based on an old paradigm of job hierarchy and progressive responsibility.

In contrast, modern workforce initiatives such as group collaboration, consensus decision-making, and matrix work environments are not grounded in hierarchies. These workplace styles are not compatible with old-style Level 1, Level 2 classification. The current public service position-and-level system has become an impediment to career advancement, and you won't find the same problem in most workplaces in the Real World.

Job training is also affected. In the public service, you don't get the opportunity to try your skills at a higher-level activity unless it can be done within the confines of a "developmental opportunity." These developmental opportunities cost the employer money, because under the strict regime a Level 3 employee doing a Level 4 activity must be remunerated at the Level 4 pay rate. The result is that the government can only hand out developmental opportunities when they have budgeted for the cost ahead of time.

Kyle is very glad to be free of that system.

"Unions are a necessary evil," he says, "and when they're not necessary, they're just evil." Kyle concedes that they do have value in some situations, but the negatives out-weigh the positives.

"They foster a defensive attitude," he says, "Always confrontational. It's not a healthy environment to work in."

Interesting, the unions of the public service of Canada continue to insist that government employees are all hard done by, despite the fact that their collective agreements offer them more benefits than many similar agreements in the private sector. They continue to try to negotiate for more of everything—more sick leave days, more types of leave, more advantages to the employees at the expense of the employer...who, by the way, is you in your role as taxpayer! Although I obviously believe that for many people work in the Real World is better than the public service, I don't accept that the public service is as badly oppressed as the unions claim.

The Real World operates in response to supply and demand. Except in rare cases, such as some universities and colleges, and the odd corporate entity, the white-collar world in the private sector is free of union influence. It doesn't freeze the salary for a particular skill across all employment units, nor does it need to find some extra money in the budget to give you an opportunity to try something more challenging than your current work.

One of the strongest arguments for working outside of government as a professional is the ability to work in a union-free environment.

Salary Tied to Performance

What a concept! A better job might mean a better reward.

At Kyle's organization, a portion of his annual salary bonus is tied to whether his work has met or exceeded expectations for the previous year. Better performance means better reward. It's not a bonus that's taken for granted, either. Unlike the public service, where salary and benefits are 100% fixed by a salary grid, the public sector bonus can add a substantial amount to the year-end paycheque for some people and not show up at all for others.

It's true that the government supports a variety of employee recognition programs. These are intended to compensate for the fact that they don't have the freedom to reward employees the way the private sector can. These recognition programs may include some kind of award, or gift card, or public acknowledgement of contribution in a ceremony, but because public funds are being spent the cost of the reward must necessarily be kept to a modest level.

In the Real World, employers have the freedom to reward you in a variety of ways when you do a good job. You can be

+ promoted to a higher salaried position

- given a larger office or a fancy desk
- awarded with a bonus payment
- flown to another city for a vacation
- allocated extra vacation time
- provided with a corporate credit card and entertainment budget
- assigned a company vehicle

or any combination of the above.

Even better, employers can do this on a project-by-project basis. They might decide that a particular project was so successful that the people working on it deserve a week off, or a lavish dinner paid for by the company, or a special gift. They can do as many "one-offs" as they like. They are not constrained by the public service approach that insists, "If everyone can't have it, then no one can have it."

In fact, sometimes you can even negotiate some of the rewards as a replacement for salary. If having an extra week's vacation or a company car is more important to you than the extra salary, that may be an option for you. You can negotiate that arrangement with your employer, and the fact that someone else at your level does not have the same arrangement will not be an impediment.

Grooming a Successor

A major advantage to working in the Real World is that it's acceptable to be "groomed" for a position. Grooming happens when someone thinks that you have very good potential, and is willing to spend the time and energy to mentor and train you to ensure that you have all the skills necessary to take the position over when you are ready.

For example, a manager might look at you and say, "You know, you have all the technical know-how for this job, but you need more accounting knowledge and more experience supervising staff." Based on that advice, if you take those courses and gain that experience, you may eventually get the job.

Those of you outside the civil service reading this may find it strange that employees can't be groomed for a position in the civil service. The practice is banned because it is considered to be unfairly favouring one candidate over another. It's an approach that's the exact opposite of the Real World.

> In the Real World, you can be groomed for a specific position

In the Real World, when we know somebody has the skills and potential for a given position, we've identified their gaps, arranged for them to train up on those missing skills, and guided them with judgment and decision-making over the years, we hire them.

In the public service, an employer who is aware of those same elements of grooming **can't directly hire** that individual. The best they are allowed to do is to let them compete for the job with everybody else. In many competitions, they're not even allowed to ask the candidate a question that relies on information gained from having done that specific job, because that is considered giving an unfair advantage to the incumbent.

Strange, isn't it? When it comes to elected officials in the political arena we know that the incumbent almost always has an advantage over new arrivals. The position is the incumbent's to lose, and the new arrivals must prove themselves superior if they are to unseat them. Yet when we take the political arena and turn it into an administrative service, somebody has decided that the incumbent should have no advantage.

The result of that is that many people don't actually win competitions in the civil service for the positions that they have been doing for quite a while—not because they weren't doing a good job, but because the selection board is required to ignore the fact that they were doing a good job to avoid penalizing the other candidates who didn't have the opportunity to do that job.

If the public service approach seems to you to be overly rigid and flying in the face of common sense, I'd be hard-pressed to disagree.

Grooming someone for a position is common in the Real World, so much so that it has been institutionalized into apprenticeship programs, mentorship programs, and other leadership programs. These types of programs are especially valuable where the skills cannot be taught in a classroom, but must be learned either in the school of hard knocks or from somebody with wisdom and experience.

In the civil service, there are few incentives for anyone to spend time mentoring or grooming you for a position, because when the job competition is run you are no more likely to win the position than anyone else. The sad result is that without those incentives, newcomers to a field often cannot turn to a more experienced individual for training. Not only does this approach turn government succession planning into a purely academic exercise, but it holds no attraction for those people who would like to plan their careers.

Fortunately for those who want to learn their craft from a master, the Real World works differently. Grooming and mentoring is common. A leader in a field is often judged by how many other leaders they produce. People will invest in you when they can be assured of some return on investment.

The same benefit will accrue to you as you develop your career. If you have expertise in a field and you groom others to be as expert as you are, you are considered a standard-setter in the Real World. People will flock to your door to be trained by you.

Will Government Change?

Bringing on new staff in the government requires many steps, from running the position through official classification, to obtaining clearance for the hiring of a new employee, to obtaining funding, through defining a range of potential candidates, setting up selection criteria, testing, interviews, and so on. The two weeks' notice of departure usually given by an employee in the civil service can't possibly tide the employer over the six to nine months it takes to hire their replacement.

You might be led to wonder whether government will start doing things differently in the future. After all, it's going to need to attract new employees competitively with the private sector on an ongoing basis. Won't they be forced to adopt the practices that the private sector uses? Will they try to make it easier for you to advance?

Highly unlikely.

First of all, there is no shortage of people wanting to work inside the government. It could be the fact that historically a public service position was a prestigious honour, and there is some spillover of that cachet even into the modern era. It could be that people are simply drawn to a job that still offers a pension; it seems there are fewer and fewer of those these days. Whatever the reason, from the employer's point of view the government is a buyer's market: far too many candidates, far too few jobs.

Secondly, and perhaps more importantly, government has been burned too many times. In the past, there were far too many instances where senior officials hired people in a clear use abuse of power. They hired their children, nieces, nephews, neighbours, friends, old colleagues, and anyone else who needed a favour. All these favours were handed out from the public purse. Clearly these processes were neither open nor transparent, and both the civil service and the public suffered as a result.

It's not easy to punish public service employees for wrongdoing (we'll look at why that is in another chapter). In fact, it's so difficult to punish for wrongdoing that there's an enormous reluctance even to try. Instead, all the efforts are focussed on processes for prevention rather than treatment. The government philosophy has evolved to the point where people believe that it's better to have 100 steps in place to act as checks and balances against wrongdoing than to be put in the awkward position of having to slap someone's wrist.

As a result, hiring new employees—even temporary help or contractors—invokes processes that are elaborate and inflexible, and failure to follow those processes results in even more delay.

The "Fairness" Trap

In the public service, the convoluted hiring process ends up being an obstacle to career advancement. The unfortunate part is that these extensive procedures are all done in the name of "openness, transparency, and fairness."

The principle of openness is clearly defensible. If the people in power get to hire their buddies, the pool of candidates is limited. If one wasn't fortunate enough to go to the kinds of schools or institutions that the people in power went to, one is at a severe disadvantage when trying to get government work. Contracts and jobs should be open to everyone.

The principle of transparency is valid, too. If the public is to hold government to account, it must be able to inspect what government is doing. With the exception of cases involving security issues and sensitive information, processes like hiring employees and engaging contractors should be discoverable and reviewable by people who are not a party to the contract. That inspection can only be done if the process is transparent. The government's continual efforts and commitment to increase the transparency of all its internal workings are commendable.

Openness and transparency are easy to gauge because they are essentially two-dimensional concepts. Openness can be measured along a linear scale, with "open" at one end and "closed" at the other. Similarly, transparency can be measured along a linear scale, with "transparent" at one end and "opaque" at the other. In both cases, every process can be evaluated against the scale, and a minimum acceptable level set.

Fairness, in contrast, is much more problematic.

Fairness sits not on a two-dimensional line but on an uneven surface, riddled with hills and valleys. Balancing fairness is a game where we try to move a ball towards a target by tilting the surface in different directions. To force the ball to roll in a specific direction, we tip the surface, perhaps raising the left side as we lower the right side. Every upward movement creates an associated downward movement.

Just like coaxing the ball into a balanced position, rules intended to achieve fairness work by tipping the board. When we try to make things fair for one set of stakeholders, too often we do so at the expense of another.

In the public service job posting game, fairness is considered a two-dimensional instead of a three-dimensional grading—a line instead of a surface. The only axis of relevance is whether or not the process is fair to the potential candidate. If some aspect of the process is found to be unfair to a candidate then the entire process is deemed unfair.

The problem with that approach is that in addition to the candidate many more players should be considered, but all other stakeholders are completely ignored.

While we are waiting nine months for the competition process to run its course, what are we doing to be "fair" to everyone else? Is it "fair" to the manager of the vacant position that they have to spend an inordinate amount of time scrambling to ensure that the workload can be covered off, and that service levels diminish as little as possible? Is it "fair" to the people remaining in the office that an extra work burden is imposed on them, to pick up the slack created by the vacant position? Is it "fair" to the public that they must wait longer for government services as the office's output is decreased due to low staff numbers? Is it "fair" to the people tasked with the examination marking, interviewing and evaluation process of the candidates that they have to spend dozens of hours working on the hiring process when their main jobs are to handle operational features. What about this system makes it "fair" to anyone at all that our public service continually operates below capacity because an extraordinarily lengthy hiring process prevents us from bringing in staff in a timely basis?

We won't receive an answer to those questions because in the civil service it doesn't matter. Processes are so focused on fairness to the candidates that they ignore the impact the vacancies have on the operation of the different programs, the compensatory losses in other areas, or even the morale of the staff in the office during the six-month period of the hiring process.

Fairness might sound like a noble goal, but fairness along one axis is only achievable at the expense of another. We can't smooth out all the hills and valleys on our surfaces and make them flat. Aside from that being a practical impossibility, it's not defensible—it wouldn't be "fair" to those people who rely on hills and valleys!

Organizations in the Real World hire people much more quickly because they understand that taking people off their regular jobs to compensate for a vacancy during the hiring process costs the company money. They know that the process shouldn't cost more than the value of the benefit they're going to get from it. As mentioned earlier, the focus in the Real World is on results, not process.

Do you find the public service approach to advancement and job promotion to be a roadblock to your career? It might be an advantageous approach for some people, but it's not for others. If you have the ability to excel at your job, and would like to be recognized for that through career advancement, you will find the Real World more responsive.

Links to sources and other resources are available on the *Unlocking the Golden Handcuffs* web site www.goldenhandcuffs.net/

Chapter 8

DELEGATION IN THE REAL WORLD

✧ Ethan ✧

"I don't get it," said Ethan Kirkland (not his real name), a solution vendor to a number of government offices. "How can they possibly function that way?"

Ethan was clearly frustrated, and I don't blame him for being so. He was in the process of selling a product to nine different government departments, and none of them had been particularly considerate of his time. He had given the same demonstration five times in one department, and then they asked him to come in to give it a sixth time because they had a new administrative assistant who wanted to see what the others were talking about.

"They said they were going to make this decision months ago," he said, clearly exasperated. He knows that in the Real World decisions are made much faster. "What takes them so long?"

Indeed, why does it take so long to make a decision in the government?

Several factors contribute to this problem, but the relevant one for this book is the government culture against the delegation of decision-making. The fact is that all the government people Ethan had been meeting had zero power and even less authority. The best any one of them can do is send a recommendation up one level.

In fact, recommending up one level is the best most public servants can do. Depending on the office you're working in, most individuals have no actual power. For that reason, until Ethan gets the opportunity to put his product in front of somebody with a high enough level to make a decision that can stick, he's not going to get anywhere. And that slow pace of decision-making frustrates both suppliers and government workers alike.

Flexible Delegation

In private industry, it is also the case that different levels in an organization are given different levels of authority for decisions and decision-making, just as in government.

What's different is that the Real World does not take the same all-or-nothing approach to delegation. A manager can easily hand down the power to make a single decision, spend money on a single purchase, approve a single contract, etc. to an individual without having to delegate every kind of similar decision, expenditure, or approval.

In the Real World, to delegate down a decision to someone else a manager need only send a note to the subordinate saying, "Go ahead, you make the decision." It's that simple. Whenever a manager finds that they don't have time to investigate, weigh options, and make a final decision to purchase a product like Ethan's, they can easily ask one of their subordinates to make the decision. Unlike the government, the delegation of activity in most organizations need not be a formal process.

As a result, decision-making of any kind happens much faster in the Real World.

The Value of Time

Private industry understands for the most part that people's time is not free. Everyone's time is worth something, hence the old saw "Time is money."

Making you, the employee, redo work you've already done, costs money. Having somebody else redo the work that you did costs money. Re-inventing the wheel costs money.

Government doesn't understand this, and rare is the public service position that values your time. Salaries is a separate budget item from Operation and Maintenance, and the dollar spent buying a notebook is dearer than the dollar spent paying an hourly wage. The common government view is that your time is free, but the notebook costs money.

If one treats people's time as an unlimited resource, one never calculates a meeting as a dollar value spent. In that case, it's easy to have staff sit through countless vendor demos without worrying about how much it might be costing the organization, much less costing the people running the demonstration.

You are much more likely to have decisions delegated to you in the real world.

Feeling Respected

From my point of view, the greatest reward of the freedom to delegate found in private industry is that I feel trusted and respected as a professional. My opinion matters.

The absence of delegation of decision-making is a serious problem for the civil service, and one I experienced many times. In sixteen years working for the government, only once did I have a supervisor say to me, "You go ahead and decide, Lewis. I trust your judgment."

Now I know for a fact that some civil servants are fortunate enough to work for managers who do say exactly that. There are some exceptional managers who give their subordinates broad stroke instructions and let them run with their projects, asking them to use their best judgment and to rely on their professional skills. The civil servants who have those managers are very lucky indeed.

Unfortunately, the vast majority of public servants don't enjoy that luxury. Your judgment—even when it's the product of years of education and field experience—is rarely going to be trusted in a government setting. There's always somebody above you in the hierarchy who feels that their judgment is better than yours, and that you don't have the "bigger picture" in mind.

I much prefer it out in the Real World, where my judgment **is** trusted. In the Real World, decisions are delegated to me, and I make them. I use my knowledge,

---

Said rarely to anyone in the public service: "Go ahead and decide. I trust your judgment."

---

experience, and my judgment to guide my actions, and I can feel proud doing it.

Can you make decisions thoughtfully? Is your judgment trustworthy? Would you like to be able to make professional decisions within your field of expertise without having to get each one approved by your supervisor before you act on it?

If you like taking responsibility for your actions, being accountable for your work, and having the authority to make a certain number of decisions, you won't find that situation in the public service. You need to step outside its walls, in the Real World, to find that kind of environment.

Links to sources and other
resources are available on the
Unlocking the Golden Handcuffs web site
www.goldenhandcuffs.net/

Chapter 9

JOB SECURITY IN THE REAL WORLD

One of the most common reasons public servants offer for remaining with the government is that their jobs are secure.

I have three responses to that reason:

1. They're really not.
2. Jobs in the Real World are just as secure.
3. In any case, that's just an excuse meaning "I feel safe here."

The Components of Job Security

When we talk about job security, we are really referring to a combination of one or more distinct factors:

1. the organization is stable, or at least likely to exist in the foreseeable future
2. the need for the position in the organization is likely to persist in the foreseeable future
3. the engagement of the individual in the position is of an indeterminate length

4. getting rid of an employee is a process subject to rules set by contract, collective agreement, or otherwise.

Is it true that those factors guarantee the security of your job in the public service? Let's examine them individually.

1. The organization is stable

This one is true. There will always be a government.

If something happens such that we no longer have a government, then losing your job will be the least of your worries.

Moreover, government will always have lots of offices. Like the Hydra, when one head falls off three more appear in its place. If job stability to you is only about the future of your employer, then government is the place to be.

2. The position will always be needed

Usually true, but not guaranteed. Many of the positions currently held in government will likely required in the foreseeable future; however, public service history is full of surprise examples where large numbers of positions were suddenly deemed unnecessary.

Example #1: in the mid-1990s, the government was so impressed with the capabilities of micro-computers that it decided records management staff were no longer necessary. Going forward, someone thought, computers will completely organize all our information for us. (No doubt, this someone had never themselves used a computer and relied on an assistant to organize documents. Note to self: don't set policy about things you don't understand.) Most full-time record- keepers eventually went the way of the dodo.

Example #2: in the early years of the current decade, the Canadian federal government reduced its ranks by about 10% over a three year period. Some 35,000 positions were eliminated under a cost-savings program euphemistically called the Deficit Reduction Action Plan.[10] I suppose in that case you could claim that your job was at least 90% secure.

Example #3: the Canadian Government's recent "Transformation of Pay" initiative resulted in the loss of hundreds of compensation advisor jobs. Technically, most of those positions were not eliminated but instead were relocated to a small town in the Maritimes. As a practical matter, though, anyone who wasn't prepared

---

[10] Ottawa Citizen: GC job cut: http://ottawacitizen.com/news/national/federal-government-on-track-to-cut-35000-public-service-jobs

to uproot themselves and move to the new location had to start looking for other work.[11]

The situation is no different in the United States. Fortune magazine projected that the budget introduced in May 2017 by then newly-elected President Trump would lead to between 100,000 and 200,000 job cuts in the civil service.[12]

3. The individual is an indeterminate employee

True to a point. An "indeterminate employee," in the lingo of government, contrasts with an employee hired for a fixed term such as one year or three months. In a downsizing exercise, indeterminate employees are more likely to retain their jobs than term or temporary employees.

The greater job security comes from the fact that they may not be first on the chopping block. That doesn't guarantee, however, that they won't be second or third.

---

[11] Treasury Board of Canada Secretariat: Lessons Learned from the Transformation of Pay Administration Initiative

[12] Fortune: 2017/03/16

4. Getting rid of an employee is complicated

True, but again, only to a point. There are very strict rules around firing employees in the public service. The result is that being let go takes a long time.

This factor is not a guarantee of security; it's simply a guarantee that if you're fired it won't happen quickly.

Job Loss Through Incompetence

Although people don't talk about it as much, there is one other factor that makes a public service job more secure than a private sector job: it's virtually impossible to get fired from the public service for incompetence.

I excluded this factor from the list of four above because overall it's a negative, not a positive, feature of the public service. When a bad public servant is hired, for all intents and purposes the rest of us are stuck with them for good.

As a manager in the public service, the inability to get rid of incompetent employees ended up being a severe impediment to me and my team, and made it difficult for us to meet our deliverables. In one position I had just over 30 subordinates report to me. Most were actually very good to excellent employees, but a couple of them were...um...shall we say, somewhat of a challenge.

Had it the been the private sector, we would have sent these individuals packing and replaced them with people who were of the same calibre as everyone else. But it was government, and—strange as it may seem to those from the Real World—no such option is available.

The entire framework governing employee competence dictates that the employer bears the responsibility rather than the employee. Incompetent employees were, apparently, my fault as the manager. If they were bad at their jobs it was my fault, because I didn't train them. If they didn't complete the job properly it was my fault, because I didn't fully explain what I wanted or I didn't give them the tools they needed or I hadn't documented my expectations…whatever the situation is, somehow it's not the employee's fault.

The inability to oust incompetence is a sad reality in the public service today. Powerful unions and convoluted requirements around disciplinary procedures have brought overworked managers to the point where it's simply easier to let a bad employee get away with doing bad work then to try to do something about it. In fact, the easiest way to get rid of a bad government employee is to give them a glowing review when called by a prospective employer for a reference. In this way, incompetent employees are regularly handed off to be someone else's problem.

The Real World does not suffer fools so gladly. The trash is emptied regularly.

But if you are a good employee, then fear not. Recall Lord Baden-Powell's statement: "If you make yourself indispensable to your employer, he is not going to part with you in a hurry no matter what it costs him."

Downsizing Through Attrition

As a taxpayer, I can't fault the government for cutting positions it can't afford. What is problematic, however, is that the most common approach to downsizing in the public service is loss through attrition.

Attrition relies on the fact that, over time, employees voluntarily leave their positions for one reason or another, such as finding other jobs or retirement. The positions they vacate are then not refilled. Supposedly, this approach softens the blow that would normally accompany an initiative to reduce staff.

In February, 2017 the Government of Newfoundland and Labrador announced that it was cutting a large number of jobs from the core civil service. Part of the public relations spin put on the initiative was that 30%

of those positions were already vacant.[13] Evidently, the logic was that when a vacant position is cut, no one actually loses a job. In other words, the employer tried to make the case that the attrition had already occurred, so there would be no blow to soften.

But any public servant knows better. Attrition is the **worst** way to handle downsizing. Consider the following illustration.

Assume we have an office that provides benefit cheques to half a million qualifying citizens once a month. Ten workers in the office are barely able to keep up with the demands of the workload. One day, one of the ten workers leaves the office for a job in another department. There are now nine workers servicing the same number of applicants. They are no longer able to keep up with the workload, but because of downsizing based on attrition, we don't fill that tenth position back up. Then someone retires, and we're down to eight workers. The office struggles.

For a variety of reasons, government normally doesn't bring in temporary help to cover off people's vacations, so when someone in this office goes on vacation for three weeks, we are down to seven workers. We can

---

13 CBC: Govt of NL job cuts

take preventive steps to ensure that no two people have their vacations scheduled at the same time, but we need to pray that no one gets sick.

We didn't go from ten workers to eight because we thought it was a good idea. We didn't deliberately decide to downsize. With the attrition approach, the number of people working in an office is not determined by the requirements of the workload, but by the fortuitous turn of events in the lives of the workers.

Let's take this illustration one step further. Assume that all ten workers are trained benefits administrators and that the job requires those skills. Assume also that this benefits program is not being cut and the government is committed to providing full staffing. What happens when we go from ten workers to eight and the missing employees must be replaced?

In the Real World, they'd hire two new skilled benefits administrators. Makes sense, right?

The public service does it differently. Across the hall from this program is a facilities management office which, unfortunately, was downsized from ten to five employees.

If we were to cut employees along with positions—the way they do in the Real World—then we'd end up with a situation where five employees with expertise in facilities management would be out of a job. This would be an unfortunate turn of events for those five employees, and we'd feel bad for them, but it was nothing personal. The program was cut for valid reasons and these five are casualties of the situation.

But no, reduction by attrition works differently. We now have five employees with an expertise in facilities management who need to be reallocated to other programs that weren't cut. Remember those two vacant positions in the benefits administration office? They become our way out.

So we take two facilities managers and we move them to the benefits administration office. They are now required to do work which does not leverage either their knowledge or their skill set. And what about the needs of the benefits program, whose smooth operation requires ten qualified benefits administrators? That's considered to be a matter of training—nothing that a half-day seminar and a good employee manual can't solve.

During the Deficit Reduction Action Program in 2012/13, managers were advised to allow downsized employees who had been reassigned to them two years to train up into their positions. Put differently, the eight workers in the benefits application office—who were total bystanders throughout the entire incident—are now expected to pick up the slack for two years until the new people can come up to speed.

The notion of fairness was raised back in chapter 7 with respect to hiring practices, but the question is just as valid here: for whom exactly is this process fair? The five facilities managers who are moved into new areas, who need to retrain and do not get to work in their field of expertise? The eight benefits administrators who are now doing the work of ten? The manager of the benefits administration unit, who is now responsible for training two brand new people as well as keeping the unit output at the same level? How about the citizens who may have their benefit cheques delayed because the rules of attrition say that we do not hire new outside people into positions when there are current employees who are looking for work?

The answer, of course, is that downsizing through attrition is fair to none of these people. The only people that this process can be said to be fair to are the two people who left voluntarily, creating the job vacancies in the first place.

Accountability and Delegation

The resistance to the delegation of decision-making discussed in a previous chapter is clearly related to the inability to fire people.

The general principle of corporate accountability holds the people at the top of a pyramid responsible for outcomes.

In the Real World, people at the top are prepared to take on this accountability because they are not hamstrung when it comes to staffing. They have the freedom to hire the people they need to do the job. They build their teams knowing the skills and competencies of the people they have hired. Finally, they have the ability to let someone go when they fail to meet expectations without months of procedures intervening.

In the public service, managers are not permitted to choose their teams. They inherit whomever is working there at the time, and they do not have the freedom to hire and fire to help fill their needs. As a result, they are

> Real World managers can influence the make-up of their teams

not in a position to trust that decisions below them are being made the way they would like them to.

The ability of managers in the Real World to influence who sits on their teams improves the likelihood of their success. If you enjoy managing people, but feel that working in the public service you haven't been given the right people to manage, you may find management in the Real World an easier go. You may also find that you are far more likely to delegate decisions to subordinates, because you have more control over who stays and who goes.

Similarly, when you are hired in the Real World by somebody who understands your skills and who trusts your judgment, you will find that you are given a lot more decision-making authority then you could ever be accorded in the public service. That decision-making authority is rewarding in and of itself.

No Job Is Truly Secure

What if you're a good, competent employee? If you keep your nose to the grindstone, follow instructions, and are loyal to the public service, in that case aren't you comparatively safe?

✧ Suzanne ✧

Try asking Suzanne van Fenema (not her real name), who dedicated 21 years to the same program in a government health department. With only six months to go before she reached that magic age where she could retire without a pension penalty, she found herself in the midst of an initiative by senior management to replace current workers with a whole new staff.

Suzanne was an exemplary employee. In 21 years she had not received one negative performance review. She had never been told that her work was not up to par, nor given any other indication that management was unhappy with her for any reason.

One day, seemingly out of the blue, a new senior management team took over and decided to take a different approach to the program she was working in. Her manager called her in to the office and pulled no punches, telling her that her current position was being rewritten. The revised job description was expected to be so different from the current one that Suzanne wouldn't qualify for it. The manager suggested that Suzanne would be better off resigning immediately, rather than going through the indignity of not being able to keep her position.

Suzanne quietly indicated that she had no intention of resigning, at which point the Director became bluntly clear: "If you don't retire, we can 'performance manage' you out of your job."[14]

The threat was not empty. Almost immediately Suzanne started to notice that she was being given assignments that seemed intended to fail. A four-week report due in three days. A comparative environmental scan with a last minute change in the factors to be examined. Critical points left out of instructions. And so on.

It seemed clear that management was determined to get its way and move her out before her time was up. This was not the way Suzanne expected to be ending a 21-year career in public service.

Disadvantages of Job Security

The problem with job security, of course, is that even bad employees get job security. The lazy employee gets it. The employee who picks only the plum tasks and leaves the less desirable work for everyone else gets it. The employee who screws up every job gets it. The employee who wastes hours surfing the Internet gets it. Everyone gets it.

---

[14] The phrase is industry-speak meaning "we can set performance objectives that you won't be able to meet."

When everybody has job security, the quality of the workforce is noticeably lower than it is in a workplace that doesn't offer that perk. A workplace that rewards performance and competence with continued employment will, over time, accumulate more high-performing and competent employees than a workplace that keeps anyone meeting the absolute minimum standards of acceptability.

Let's turn this around. Which organization would you rather work for: one that retains people because they do great work, or one that retains them because a collective agreement gives them no choice?

Links to sources and other
resources are available on the
Unlocking the Golden Handcuffs web site
www.goldenhandcuffs.net/

Chapter 10

LEADERSHIP IN THE REAL WORLD

We should avoid the mind-numbing habit of assuming we are so much wiser than our superstitious, bigoted ancestors that we don't even have to study history to avoid their laughably repellant mistakes. When medieval or Enlightenment chief executives [made bad decisions]... it was rarely from deliberate malice. Mostly it was belief that they had a broader, less selfish vision of administrative efficiency, the public good and the welfare of individuals. Exactly as it is today.

~ John Robson
Film-maker, Columnist and Commentator

I'm prepared to work from the assumption that the leadership in the government is well-intentioned. People want to do good, not bad. Even if for only ego-tistical reasons, people want their projects to succeed, not to fail.

Yet so many government projects do fail, with unsettling predictability. Why?

To a very large degree, we have a problem with accountability in the public service. Much has been written on this subject, and how it can be rectified.[15] I won't belabour the issue to the extent that it isn't relevant to our subject here, but I want to mention a few noteworthy points.

Accountability

The Real World does two things better than the public service when it comes to accountability.

The first is that it actually assigns it. Well-run projects in the Real World are designed in a way that assigns responsibility not only for key deliverables, but for key processes.

In the public service, they tend to ignore accountability for processes, and focus almost entirely on responsibility for producing deliverables. That omission can be fatal to a large project. Failure to set up proper accountabilities for the Transformation of Pay Administration project has

---

[15] See, for example, Kevin Page, *Unaccountable: Truth and Lies on Parliament Hill* (2015)

been determined to be one of the main causes of the Phoenix disaster.[16]

The second, and more important, difference is that accountability is not assigned without concomitant authority.

A Google search of the phrase "accountability without authority" leads to numerous articles explaining that giving managers the first without the second is the recipe to quick burnout. Without decision-making power, the manager basically becomes a slave to the person giving orders.

Government has honed this recipe to a science. The policies and documents they produce are replete with sections on Roles and Responsibilities (which are actually two distinct things although one would never know it from those documents). These sections list all the activities, duties, and outcomes that various parties are responsible for. None of this responsibility, though, comes with any authority; the authority is reserved for one or two individuals or committees at the very top of the hierarchy.

---

[16] Lessons Learned from the Transformation of Pay Administration Initiative

In the Real World, an assignment of responsibility would include the authority to make specific decisions relevant to those responsibilities. Your role thereby becomes significantly more sound, and your deliverables more achievable.

Reporting Up

Reporting to one's superiors on progress is a critical component of any ongoing operation if it is to monitor its successes and its shortcomings. The value gained from any specific reporting exercise is directly dependent on the quality of the information in the report.

Government has an aversion to reporting bad news on operations up the chain of command. In the public service, bad news will be spun and rewritten to make it more palatable to the level receiving it.[17]

That means that often the reports are meaningless when they move up the ranks. This is especially the case when the immediate goal of launching on time and within budget is more important than the ultimate goal.[18]

---

[17] Lessons Learned from the Transformation of Pay Administration Initiative

[18] *ibid.*

You won't find that kind of effort directed to hiding or fudging the results of bad news in the private sector. In the Real World, reporting operational achievements up to higher levels is generally an exercise in relaying the truth. Unless someone is using subterfuge to hide their own failures or illegitimate activities, people are eager to report reality to senior management. If the news is good, there may be a reward; if the news is bad, the report may draw attention to the problems and someone might step up to help fix them.

As one would expect, the agreed-upon key performance indicators for the bottom line success in the private sector are financial. Even when they're achieving some major social goal, such as cleaning up air pollution or reducing poverty, companies can pat themselves on the back only when their actions are financially sustainable. A corporation that raises its prices beyond what the market can support will not be successful, no matter how noble the social goal motivating it.

We've already talked about how government can't fall back on profit figures to prove success. That being the case, other performance metrics are required. These need to be the kinds of numbers that will impress people. When meaningful numbers can't be found, the reporting resorts to meaningless ones, which is why we see counts of things like hits on a Web page to measure usefulness, or software licences purchased to measure user adoption. When one has no choice but to show a good news picture, having some numbers is better than no numbers.

Large-Scale Projects

Government has long had a problem managing large-scale projects. Examples are just too easy to find:

✦ the failed new pay system, Phoenix, which was budgeted originally at $310 million but whose remedial costs have so far been forecast at an additional $400 million, and are still climbing[19]

✦ the consolidation of information technology infrastructure centres into the single entity called Shared Services Canada, currently over three years delayed and used by only 15% of the intended target group[20]

✦ the Canada.ca portal, designed to merge 1,500 Web sites into a single one, years behind schedule and ten times over budget[21].

---

[19] CBC Investigates. http://www.cbc.ca/news/canada/ottawa/phoenix-government-psac-payroll-1.4300801

[20] CBC: RCMP to develop own e-mail system because of government delays.

[21] CBC: Federal government's Canada.ca project 'off the rails.'

These examples might seem all relatively recent, but government projects have been failing on a large scale for a very long time.

For most of its history, the Government of Canada allowed different departments considerable leeway in running their own affairs. Compensation, information technology, facilities, and many other administrative services were run separately by each department.[22]

Large-scale projects until recently, therefore, were departmental, and so when they failed, it wasn't as news-worthy because the scale was much smaller. It's only since whole-of-government initiatives started working their way across multiple departments that the dollar figures shot up so high.

In addition, failures today are less likely to remain hidden. Recent initiatives in Open Government have opened up the file drawers and revealed many docu-ments that were not made available around previous projects.

This is not to say that projects never fail in the private sector. On the contrary, projects fail all the time, run into cost overruns, delays, and enormous amounts of

[22] Treasury Board of Canada Secretariat: Lessons Learned from the Transformation of Pay Administration Initiative

resistance. The failures cost people lots of time, money, and inconvenience.

But failed projects in the public sector differ from those in the private sector in four major ways.

The first is the most obvious: private sector projects that fail lose their own money; whereas, failed projects in the public sector lose money that comes from tax-payers. When a government project fails, there might be some embarrassment around it, but there are always taxpayers to pull more money from. We know that the amount of care taken around public spending falls below the standard of care that people use when spending their own money. Private corporations, which risk losing their own money, take greater care and are less likely to fail.

The second difference is that in the private sector, people actually lose their jobs for failing to do good work. When one's job security depends on the success of the project, one takes a lot more care when making decisions.

The third is that in the private sector decisions around major projects are made solely for financial reasons. When the project starts costing more than it saves, the project is cut.

Lastly, private industry has a better understanding of the fallacy of sunk costs. The sunk cost fallacy happens when one adds costs-to-date to future costs to come up with a total figure against which to determine validity of the project. When deciding whether or not to proceed with a project on any given day, the **only** relevant question to ask is the following: "Is the amount of money we are going to spend **from this point on** outweighed by the amount of income or savings or benefit that we will get from this in the future?"

As eloquently explained by author David McRaney,

> Sunk costs are a favorite subject of economists. Simply put, they are payments or investments which can never be recovered. An android with fully functioning logic circuits would never make a decision which took sunk costs into account, but you would. As an emotional human, your aversion to loss often leads you right into the sunk cost fallacy.[23]

The sunk cost fallacy leads one to say, "we've already spent x thousand dollars on this, so it would be a waste not to spend the next y thousand dollars to finish the project."

The temptation to include sunk costs in decisions around projected costs is especially strong in government,

---

[23] McRaney, David: *You Are Not So Smart, 2011*

where officials risk losing face if it looks like taxpayers' money has been spent wrongly in the past. Whereas private industry would stand up and declare aloud, "we are not going to throw good money after bad,"—exactly the way you might do when examining your own finances—no one in the government is going to admit that money thrown was ever bad. What is considered a sound decision in private industry is in fact a career limiting move in the public sector.

Absence of Real Consequences

The coach of a hockey team that loses too many games may be unceremoniously dismissed one day, with little warning. In the Real World there are consequences for poor performance, unlike the situation in government where, as discussed in an earlier chapter, poor performers simply get shunted off to other areas. The cultural bias that keeps an organization from firing rank-and-file employees no matter how poor their performance is just as potent when it comes to senior management.

> The private sector falls prey to the "sunk costs" fallacy less often

That senior executives in the government who have committed major blunders are not held accountable in most cases is incontestable. Pick any scandal at random and look into whether or not someone was disciplined for errant behaviour or poor judgment. At most, we will find a token disciplinary action taken against one or two individuals, and we will have to dig to find that because those disciplinary actions are not publicized.

Those actions are not very disciplinary, either. A well-known tactic for dealing with ineffectual top executive personnel is to give them a "special assignment." That puts them somewhere where they can't do any more damage but do not suffer the indignity of a job loss.

Simply by virtue of the fact that the Real World sets standards for performance of upper management and does not tolerate incompetence as generously, the Real World has a higher quality of upper management over-all. It only makes sense: private industry filters people out at two stages: intake and performance review; government only filters out at intake.

Management Training

Can the leadership in the government improve? Yes, of course, If they wanted to. Extensive training is available to people at the senior levels of the government, but most of them don't want it. Most of them think that by the time they've reached the senior levels they don't need a coach.

"This is a sharp contrast with private industry," notes Simon Beauchemin (not his real name). Simon was a senior consultant at several well-known large organizations for a number of years. In 2015 he ventured into the civil service, and began working in a central agency. "Everybody who works can use a coach," he says, "and the higher up you go in the hierarchy of an organization, the more you need one."

In the Real World, executives at the top of an organization get a lot of coaching.

"They want that coaching," says Simon. "They know that they can't handle everything alone, and they reach for business experts and other professionals to help them deal with the types of challenges that executives face."

"But it's exactly the opposite in the public sector," he notes sadly. "Senior management in the government

> Real World executives are more
> open to coaching

takes comparatively little advantage of coaching. People reach the level of director and think they know everything."

"Managers in government think that accepting coaching is admitting that they aren't capable of doing their jobs," Simon sees the contrast clearly.

"It's a totally different psyche from the senior management in the private sector."

Are you looking for a good work environment? Good senior management is the most critical influence on that work environment, and you are more likely to find good senior management in the Real World.

"Because of this continued emphasis on coaching and personal improvement," Simon explains, "the quality of senior managers in the private sector far outshines that in the public sector."

Simon also acknowledges the benefits of having multiple filtering stages, and not just relying on the intake process.

"In general, bad managers in the private sector don't last too long. They are found out quickly and the Human Resources branch takes responsibility for weeding out the bad apples. That just doesn't happen in the public sector."

In summary, the Real World has three cultural features that work together to produce a vastly superior level management than what you'll find in the private sector: truly holding people accountable for their actions, an openness to coaching for skill improvement, and the support for more than one filtering mechanism.

Would you like to learn from real leaders? Would you like to see people in action who have a vision, who can articulate it, motivate their employees, and challenge you to be the best you can be?

Again, I can also turn the question around: would you rather work for someone whose job depends on them performing well, or for someone who has tenure and immunity?

Links to sources and other
resources are available on the
Unlocking the Golden Handcuffs web site
www.goldenhandcuffs.net/

Chapter 11

BUREAUCRACY IN THE REAL WORLD

Government may, for some people, be the dictionary definition of *bureaucracy*. But let's be fair: every large organization needs to have a certain amount of bureaucracy in order to function. Satirist Scott Adams, the creator of the Dilbert® comic strip, has built a very successful career out of his ability to highlight the more entertaining idiocies of corporate sector bureaucracy.

To a certain extent, bureaucracy is the same in the Real World as it is in the government. Expect to experience the same frustration in both worlds: things that should take you a few minutes end up taking days. Things that should be simple end up getting complicated. Expect to be asked repeatedly to provide information that you've already given, including information not actually necessary to delivering you the service. Do they really need my postal code to respond to my e-mail request?

Bureaucracy is predictable in its approach: Procedures are sacrosanct. Special cases will not be accommodated without a great deal of fuss. Someone will tell you that the process cannot be changed, and if you press them on it, you'll learn that it can be changed but needs to go through four committees. The system will break in the middle and no one will notice except you. And to cap it all off, most people ignore why a given rule was first put in place, and will follow it slavishly even when it is totally unnecessary.

What's the same

Just so we're all on the same page, I'm using the term *bureaucracy* to refer to a set of conditions that includes the following:

Rigid controls and processes

It starts out well-intentioned. Based on sensible goals like achieving standardization, economizing resources, or controlling finances, processes serve as oversight mechanisms. If everybody in an organization could go out and buy a new piece of technology whenever they wanted to, maintaining the resultant mosaic of hardware would strain the financial, technical, and human resources of the organization.

Procedures function by interposing a series of checks and balances. Requests for specific actions need to trigger specific steps, and the checks and balances ensure that the needs of the organization are taken into account along the way.

Paperwork

Whether on old-fashioned carbon-paper–based triplicate forms, or digitized into a series of mouse-clicks, paperwork refers to the ongoing capture and relay of information required by the procedures. Included are the capture of approvals from specific individuals—usually evidenced by signatures, ink or electronic—and creating an audit trail.

Paperwork is necessary for transparency. The people who come after the event need to be able to see the evidence that the procedure was followed. Without an audit trail there can be no accountability.

What's different

There are some differences of note.

Because the government expenditure comes from the public purse, it has a higher duty of care when it comes to ensuring value for money. If a private organization wastes money, they alone feel the pain. When the government wastes money, every taxpayer feels the pain. This higher duty of care has raised the bar on due diligence.

Moreover, governments have been burned in the past by an excess of abuses of power. For many years, nepotism was rampant in the procurement and hiring world, and lavish spending on comfort items was uncontrolled. Kudos to government for trying to improve on these problems, but the result has been a significantly larger collection of processes and controls, all of which are very rigid. That makes navigating the bureaucracy of government much more difficult than in the Real World.

A Culture Focussed Entirely on Prevention

As mentioned earlier in this book, it is very difficult to fire someone in the public sector, in contrast with the Real World where we can simply get rid of someone we don't want. Similarly, punishment in the public sector is a long and arduous process; it is much easier to punish people for wrongdoing in a non-union environment.

In the absence of recourse to quick punishment, all the efforts in the public service have been focussed on prevention. The prevailing philosophy is, "a pound of prevention makes up for having no cure." As a result, every single check and balance that could possibly block a wrongdoing is built into the system.

In the Real World, attention is paid both to prevention and to enforcement. Were someone to cheat the system, for example, to spend $25,000 to purchase a piece of equipment outside of the procurement process, they would be fired. Then the follow-up response to the problem in the Real World would be one of two approaches: either (1) change something in the procurement process to ensure that it won't happen again, or (2) change something in the enforcement process to ensure that more violators will be caught.

In the Real World the violators can be punished, so it makes sense to try to catch them. In the public service, they don't punish anyone, so there's no point in catching violators. All the resources are put into prevention, and as a consequence, public service procedures tend to be longer and less flexible. You will likely find that procedures take less time in the private sector.

In addition, the Real World doesn't take the preventive or the enforcement approaches to extremes. In the Real World someone first balances the costs of the checks and balances against the costs of abuse. Unlike government, which might put a process in place that costs $10,000 to ensure that someone doesn't misspend $100 on a purchase of office supplies, most private organizations have a sense of scale. Since the goal of the private organization is to maximize profit, checks and balances that cost more than the savings are an unwelcome interference.

The bottom line is that you cannot escape bureaucracy by moving to the private sector. What you will find, however, is that organizations in the Real World take a more moderate approach to bureaucracy, because (1) they are only accountable to themselves and not in danger of wasting public funds, and (2) they are not afraid to kick enforcement mechanisms into action when they are required.

Links to sources and other resources are available on the *Unlocking the Golden Handcuffs* web site www.goldenhandcuffs.net/

Chapter 12

THE EXTERNAL SHACKLES

Breaking free from your current situation involves releasing yourself from two sets of shackles: external and internal.

The external shackles are those prizes dangled in front of public servants to disincentivize them from leaving. The internal shackles are the fears and insecurities that you bring to the table, and that hinder your thought process as you evaluate the elements of job change. We'll examine the internal shackles in the next chapter.

The external shackles include the remuneration, job stability, and opportunity. You are urged to believe that public service compensation bundle is so rich that you will never find the equivalent elsewhere.

Salary and Benefits

From an employee's perspective, remuneration comes as a package. The salary is the core piece, and with it can come other financial incentives such as medical benefits, drug plans, dental benefits, various forms of insurance and so on. Financial perks can also include services like free parking, discounted pricing for fitness clubs, on-site daycare, and other offerings that help improve your quality of life.

The main objection I hear from people who are afraid to leave the public service is that they won't earn the same amount of money out in the Real World. They are convinced that salaries are lower in the private sector. But is that really true?

Lynn Cameron is a consultant in Human Resources specializing in compensation. She doesn't believe in over-generalizing.

"Sometimes that's true and sometime it's not," she says. "It really depends on the discipline."

We've already talked in this book about how the Real World is reactive to market forces in a way that the public service is not. Depending on which direction the cycle of supply and demand is moving, it can definitely be to your advantage to have a job in the private sector.

One thing is for sure: when the cycle changes, the public service never leads the change; they always lag behind it. Cameron recommends that you not make assumptions about salaries at any given time.

"You need to do some research to determine whether it applies in your own field," she counsels.

✧ Lori ✧

Lori Collins worked a number of years at a large national bank and a large national IT consulting firm before she made the move over to government. She doesn't regret it, but she doesn't fool herself about the salary level, either.

"If I had stayed at the bank I would be a lot better off financially than I am now," she states emphatically. She's looking at the broad financial picture, not just the wage scale.

"I don't think that working for government is as great as people make out. The benefits in the private sector are much better."

Lori admits that some old recordings were still playing in her head when she first left the private sector.

"I think there is an illusion that landing a government job is the end-all-be-all," she said. "That is a holdover from our parents' generation where opportunities were limited and government provided a good pay cheque and stability. But I see government now as being very tricky."

Lori is ready to move back to the private sector. She doesn't regret her time in government, because it gave her a wide breadth of experience. She understands now that the reality of working in a government job is harsher than the fantasy, and she's ready to go back to the Real World.

Lori is sensitive to the people she's leaving behind. "I didn't want my old public service colleagues to see this last move as a rejection," she says. "It's not about moving away from them, it's about moving toward something better."

Retirement Pension

Ah, that pension! It must be the pot at the end of the rainbow; otherwise, why would everybody be scrambling to get a job with a pension? In the public service, the pension is the bouquet of roses handed to you as soon as you reach the finish line.

But is it possible that the pension is overrated? We need to take a step back and look at the larger picture, before we can decide whether we're being offered a pot of gold.

As with any financial planning tool, a pension is designed to bestow specific benefits on specific people in specific situations. You need to examine a whole range of factors before you are in a position to make an informed decision on whether retaining the pension is to your benefit. Look at the breadth of that range.

1. Personal Circumstances

Everyone's situation is different. Whether the pension is good in your circumstances depends on many details, such your current age, the number of years you expect to work, the age at which the pension kicks in, your marital status, and whether you have dependants. Other relevant details are the state of your health, your spouse's health, and your expectations around the lifestyle you plan to have.

These details taken together form the big picture of your future, and no examination of the appropriateness of a pension can be done without gauging it against them. As you consult various experts for their advice on your pension given your personal circumstances, make sure that they see your big picture, too, and are not focused simply on crunching numbers.

2. Financial and Employment Circumstances

Your financial circumstances, both current and projected, are also part of the big picture. These circumstances include your other assets and obligations; the availability of income and benefits from a spouse; and other sources of income such as rental income, royalties, and inheritance. Financial experts will also explore your level of tolerance for risk.

What comes next for you? Are leaving the civil service to take a job somewhere else or to live a life of leisure? Maybe you're leaving to start that business that you always wanted to have.

3. Pension Terms and Benefits

The terms of every pension are different. Some are based on a defined contribution; others on a defined benefit. Your pension may or may not include health coverage, disability insurance, life insurance, and other benefits. Some pensions are indexed for inflation; others are not.

Depending on your personal circumstances, the terms of a pension may or may not work in your favour, but you can only know that by learning what the terms are.

The restrictions of different pensions vary, for example, the payout may or may not be affected by your retiring before a certain age, or having worked a certain number of years with the same employer. Investigate this aspect carefully, so you get the facts correct: some pension plans set the payout according to the date you leave your employment, whether or not you actually collect the benefit right from the time you leave. Others use the date you start collecting the payment, so you are not penalized if you leave the job but wait a number of years before drawing funds.

4. Tax Regimes

Where you live determines how your pension income will be taxed. Your taxation level, as I'm sure you already know, will also be affected by your other income, allowable deductions, tax-saving investment vehicles, and a whole slew of variables, all of which if listed here would add ten pages to this book and be painfully tiresome to read.

Assessing Your Pension

Bruce Bartleman, B.Comm CFP CLU, is an independent financial advisor who teaches people how to make sound choices around money management, especially when it comes to retirement planning. He agrees that too many people make blanket statements like, "I can't give up my pension" without being able to back those claims up with evidence.

"In each case," he says, "we need to determine the value of a given pension for a given individual in a given set of circumstances considering their tax position."

In other words, before you decide that your pension is the only life-raft to cling to as a way to sustain you postemployment, you owe it to yourself to do your due diligence and research the facts. You cannot know that your pension is irreplaceable in the absence of research and advice from knowledgeable experts.

I can't emphasize the word *expert* enough here. You're looking for people who are unbiased, trustworthy, and who have some breadth and depth of experience. These people can advise you with a perspective different from that of the employer and pension provider. You should be seeking input from your personal financial advisor, your lawyer, your accountant, and anyone else whom you rely on for retirement planning.

"People understand the need to evaluate a home against their own circumstances before purchasing it," Bartleman points out. "Even though you don't get a choice of pension, you're still looking at whether it's a good fit. The same evaluation process against your unique circumstances is necessary to see if what the plan offers will actually provide the best value when you decide to retire."

Is the Pension Worth Staying For?

If we put your pension on one side of the equation, what goes on the other side? What can you replace the pension with? When you get down to basics, a pension is simply a form of forced savings. The question you should ask is, given the four factors above, can you replicate the results of your pension through other methods, like proactive savings and sound financial planning?

Kurt Lucier, CFA, is a financial advisor who specializes in building wealth and retirement income strategies. He himself left a job that came with a pension to pursue a career that would be more rewarding.

"There's no magic to a pension," he explains. "Pension fund administrators mostly have access to the same types of investments that other investors have access to. Some pensions are particularly well run and have made some very good investments. In a few cases, due to the size of the pension funds they have been able to make investments that might be out of reach for smaller investors, such as buying a sports team.

"But it's the status of the pension fund that counts, not the number of contributors," he continues. "A large pension fund is meaningless in itself; you need to know whether its assets actually exceed its current and future liabilities. Most pension funds in the developed world are actually underfunded."

In fact, taking about a pension "fund" is in itself a fiction. Many pensions, such as the one in the Government of Canada, are administered in a "pay-as-we-go" manner. There is no separate, identifiable bank account earmarked as the "Public Service Pension Fund Account." It exists merely as an accounting entry—a liability that needs to be accounted for in the government's budget. Until the pension monies are one day actually set aside in trust, that liability is a simply a nuisance that each government perpetually passes on to the next.

Lucier acknowledges that a government pension can be a sweet deal.

"If the pension is indexed to inflation, someone starting work at 30 and sticking with the same employer until 60 can build up a very nice nest egg."

The question, however, is not whether getting a pension is a good deal, but whether the same results can be replicated in the absence of a pension. Lucier believes that it's very doable. Instead of committing yourself to 30 years with the same employer, giving the employer your money, and letting the employer do the investing, you can take matters into your own hands.

"If you saved just over 20% of your gross annual salary —being approximately your RRSP limit—and invested prudently, your results would come very close. Obviously, the decision to leave gets harder as you accumulate more time with the employer, because you've gone much farther down the rabbit hole. Someone with only ten years remaining of a target 30 would have a much more difficult time replicating the results for those last ten years."

Lucier shares my view, however, that while a good pension is a perk of a job that you love, it is no reason to stay at a job that you don't.

"I would never encourage anyone to continue down the path that continues to make them miserable," he says. "Your goal should not be to accept being miserable until you're 60, and then retire and start enjoying life. That is no way to live!"

Job Stability

We discussed job security at length in chapter 9. Despite the reality of the government's approach to downsizing, some people continue to think of it as an immutable fact, and as a situation that can't be found elsewhere.

Make no mistake—job stability anywhere is an illusion. In the mid-nineties, the country was able to recover from years of recession. It did so in a manner described by the media as a "jobless recovery." Private sector jobs that had been lost over the previous decade did not return, and the public sector fared no better. In a matter of just three years, 45,000 public service jobs were eliminated; whole departments were wiped out.[24]

Possibility of Advancement

The final enticement to stay in the public service is the possibility of career advancement.

People want to improve their lot in life, and that usually means earning more money. Naturally, they look for ways they can move up in the organization. Because government tends to be large and has a steady turnover of employees, it's easy to be tantalized by the thought that a number of high positions are waiting to be filled.

Some people will move up to senior positions, for sure, but don't put all your eggs in this basket.

For one thing, senior opportunities are relatively few and far between. Like a school system that employs a sea of teachers but only a sprinkling of principals, there will always be proportionately fewer positions available as you ascend the ladder.

---

[24] A Coming of Age: Counselling Canadians for Work in the Twentieth Century

Secondly, government has tightened its belt during the financial downturn of the last few years, and one of the cost-cutting measures is the elimination of management positions. Far more dollars can be saved by cutting a senior position than by cutting a junior one. Going forward, senior positions will continue to be scarce.

Finally, the realities of bureaucracy interfere. The more candidates vying for a position, the longer it takes to run each of them through the process. To reduce the number of hours spent on evaluating candidates, the number of potential applicants must be reduced. One of the common methods used to avoid entertaining large numbers of job applicants is to "limit the area of selection," meaning to open the position only to those currently in a specific work unit or department. Another is to ask for a specific unusual qualification or experience factor.

However it's done, to a certain degree being one of the few who land a senior position is still a matter of being in the right place at the right time. It's in no way a sure thing.

Links to sources and other
resources are available on the
Unlocking the Golden Handcuffs web site
www.goldenhandcuffs.net/

Chapter 13

THE INTERNAL SHACKLES

There are seven days in a week, and Someday isn't one of them.

~ Unknown

Wat really keeps so many unhappy public servants from leaving their jobs is not the intellectual factors discussed in the previous chapter, but the emotional ones. Doubt, anxiety, skepticism, resignation...they are all possible obstacles to clear thinking.

When I was a public servant, I asked my colleagues why they put up with being unhappy in their jobs instead of looking elsewhere. The most common response was, "I've gotten used to the way government works. It's not a problem for me anymore." Interesting. Let's add denial to that list of obstacles.

In reality, when you go right down to the source, the internal shackles are composed of fear in various forms: fear of failure, fear of pain, fear of loss, fear of regret.

Add to that list the fear of change, the fear of the unknown, and the fear of taking risks, and the result is a complete framework of fear-related reasons to stay put in a bad situation.

Kyle, our application infrastructure analyst who moved into the Real World after five years of public service, spoke candidly about his reluctance to make a jump.

"In retrospect, I was just afraid to leave," he says. "I imagined the risks to be a lot greater than they really are."

It didn't help that Kyle didn't receive much support from his peers. Most of them thought he was crazy to leave the confines and security of a government job to jump to the private sector. When he eventually found his new position, a number of similarly unhappy colleagues watched him go, wishing they could be brave enough to do the same.

There's no need to wish. They, too, can leave the public service at any time to do work they would really love. All they need to do first is overcome their fear.

The Right Time to Leave

That was a trick heading! There is no "right time to leave." If you wait until the right time approaches, you will be waiting indefinitely.

Napoleon Hill, author of *Think and Grow Rich*—one of the most popular personal development and self-improvement books of all time—speaks to this point emphatically.

"Do not wait; the time will never be 'just right,'" Hill cautioned. "Start where you stand, and work with whatever tools you may have at your command, and better tools will be found as you go along."[25]

Waiting till the time is right is a nothing more than a delay tactic. A delay tactic motivated by fear.

Renowned motivational speaker Zig Ziglar put it in succinct imagery: "If you wait until all the lights are green before you leave home, you'll never get started on your trip to the top."[26]

Read any book on career change, and you'll find the same message repeated. You don't even have to wait until **many** lights are green. You should start on your

---

[25] Napoleon Hill, *Think and Grow Rich* (1938)

[26] Zig Ziglar quotations

journey as soon as the first few lights are green. Worry about the colour of the next light when you get there.

Skill Sets

Once the public servant has moved past the initial reticence stage and is prepared to look at alternatives, their next objection is predictable: "I'm not sure what I would do if I weren't here."

I understand where that concern comes from. Not a lot of employed positions outside the civil service require expertise in reviewing welfare applications, issuing fishing permits, or preparing briefing books for House debates. Very few private companies need people to run a grants-and-contribution program, to set speed limits on highways, or to regulate a school system. The number of landowners employing their own income tax collectors has particularly dwindled somewhat since feudal times.

The bottom line is that it's unusual to find an exact match for your public service position in the private sector. As a result, you may fear that moving into the Real World

> Waiting until the time is right is a delay tactic

will highlight your limitations rather than your worth. That fear is unfounded.

Recognizing Imposter Syndrome

The first thing to note is that it's not uncommon for workers in many fields to question their own skills. In a recognized phenomenon known as *imposter syndrome*, many working individuals are haunted by an inability to internalize their accomplishments and the fear of being exposed as a "fraud" in their work.[27]

No one is immune. Newly minted doctors, lawyers, professionals of every nature well-schooled in their fields, high-ranking executives and elected officials all are prone to experiencing imposter syndrome at one point or another. It's especially common when jumping out of one's comfort zone, which includes moving from one job environment to another.

To overcome it, you need to be aware of it. Like a small stain on the cuff of your shirt, it appears much more obvious to you than to everyone else.

The same way that people who move from the private sector to government need to adjust to how things work differently, when you move in the other direction

---

[27] Wikipedia: Imposter Syndrome

you will need to make a similar adjustment. As a public servant, you have most likely been gracious and welcoming to newcomers to government, wherever they came from, and have done your best to help them fit into their new environment. People in the Real World are just as understanding and will do the same for you. There's nothing to be afraid of.

An individual leaving the government to work within a recognized field of professional expertise such as economics, science, or medicine might have it relatively easy. After all, with a university education and experience in their field, they should be able to arrive in the Real World with at least the same credibility they had when working in government.

But what about people working in fields that are not professional and recognized, and for which institutions of higher education do not offer training programs? Few public schools offer courses on how to process citizenship applications. There's no publicly recognized college diploma in licensing drivers and vehicles or in running workers compensation boards. How do public servants doing this kind of work legitimize themselves when moving to the private sector?

I won't lie to you: in some cases, it's not easy. A number of skills are required in the Real World that are often neglected by people working in the public service. You may need to bone up on some skills you haven't used in a while.

On the other hand, in many cases it's simply a challenge of simply reframing your skills. Working in government, I never thought of myself as doing "sales." Yet, clearly, there was a sales-type component to my job that I encountered every time I tried to sell a new idea to my supervisor, or to convince a committee to make a decision.

You must stop thinking of your worth as a by-product of the activities your employer has you doing today. Even if you think of yourself as simply a cog in the machinery, separate the activity you do from the skill you have. The activity might be washing widgets; the skill is knowing when they're clean enough.

Links to sources and other
resources are available on the
Unlocking the Golden Handcuffs web site
www.goldenhandcuffs.net/

Chapter 14

MAKING THE TRANSITION

I hope, now that you've reached the end of this book, that you're prepared to concede that leaving the public service to find work you really love is at least worth exploring.

If so, congratulations! You've taken the first step: opening your mind to other possibilities.

The options are endless. You can make the transition from public service to private sector as simple as a change of job, or as drastic as a change of location and lifestyle. Maybe you need an interim step between old and new, such as schooling, apprenticeship, or just some downtime to collect your thoughts. The approach that's right for you will depend on your circumstances.

It's now time to take the second step, which is to embark on a self-discovery journey and start exploring the world around you. Don't quit your current job just yet; the title of this chapter is not "Making the Break" or "Jumping In with Both Feet" (which for most people might as well be "Jumping off the Cliff").

Leaving the public service for the private sector is a transition. It needs to be first explored, then planned, and finally executed. At this point you are at the "explore" stage. Your task is to look around, look inside, and look ahead, to search for work that matches your passion.

The Rider and the Elephant

As you explore, resist using only your mind; use your heart as well.

In their book *Switch: How to Change When Change is Hard*, Chip & Dan Heath expand on a behavioural psychology model originally presented by psychologist Jonathan Haidt[28]. I have found this model to be simple yet powerful, and I'd like to share it with you here.

We are each a combination of an elephant with a rider on top. The rider represents your thinking, rational self, while the elephant represents your emotional self.

The Heath brothers elaborate:

> Perched atop the Elephant, the Rider holds the reins and seems to be the leader. But the Rider's control is precarious because the Rider is so small relative to the Elephant. Anytime the six-ton Elephant and the Rider disagree about which

[28] Jonathon Haight, *The Happiness Hypothesis: Finding Modern Truth in Ancient Wisdom*

direction to go, the Rider is going to lose. He's completely overmatched.

Most of us are all too familiar with situations in which our Elephant overpowers our Rider. You've experienced this if you've ever slept in, overeaten, dialled up your ex at midnight, procrastinated, tried to quit smoking and failed, skipped the gym, gotten angry and said something you regretted, abandoned your Spanish or piano lessons, refused to speak up in a meeting because you were scared, and so on.

People think of "willpower" as the brain directing the actions of the body despite the powerful influence of the emotions. When you see willpower in terms of the rider and the elephant, it's more like the rider trying to strong-arm the elephant into heading in a direction it doesn't want to follow. The rider can't succeed.

What's fascinating is that nobody wants to admit that their rider can't control their elephant. Whenever the elephant moves on its own, the rider instantly rationalizes the behaviour. "It's okay that I'm eating chocolate cake now because I went to the gym today," or, "I was going to do the laundry this morning, but it's okay if I don't because I'll have time on Saturday."

The Heath brothers explain that the elephant always follows a path. If you want the elephant to head in a different direction, you need either

+ to give the elephant some incentive to head in that direction, or
+ to reshape the path.

Giving the elephant an incentive means doing things like making a chore fun, or making healthy food taste delicious. The elephant responds well to a carrot and resents being driven by a stick, so it's a matter of finding the right carrots.

Reshaping the path means gaining an understanding of what makes your particular elephant react the way it does and changing the route accordingly. Does your elephant shy away from risk? Does it avoid long paths in favour of short ones? Does it need to see other elephants beside it before it will tread somewhere unknown? Just as no two riders are the same, every elephant is different and you need to learn how yours works if you're going to have any influence over it.

> Your career change must appeal to both the rider and the elephant

When you're considering a change to your life such as a change of job or career, it's insufficient to find a direction that appeals only to the rider. The path must also appeal to the elephant.

The rider has an ego that is predictably one-sided. The rider tends to blame the elephant's deviations from the path on external factors that interfere, while at the same time attributing the elephant's successes to their own competence and proficiency. Obviously, the successes as well as the failures of the elephant are attributable both to the rider and to external factors.

The more you understand your elephant, the more your career choices can take into account the needs of both the rider and the elephant.

If you're unhappy at work, or frustrated or angry or demoralized, recognize that it's the elephant who is frustrated or angry or demoralized, not the rider. The rider rationalizes the elephant's emotions based on the circumstances. "I wouldn't get so frustrated at work if my boss stopped changing his mind so often," or, "The job would be good if we only had enough staff."

Identify Your Passions

The first step in this transition is premised on your understanding of the elephant, because you need to identify what you love. What brings you joy? What makes you feel accomplished at the end of the day? What rewards you on a personal level? The rider might be supervising and running the show, but it's the elephant that brings you back day after day.

Have you truly been able to discover what will make your elephant bring you back to work every day, despite your periodic successes and failures?

Although it took me a long time, I now really understand my elephant. My passion is teaching. I love to make difficult subjects clear for people. I love when they walk out of my classroom saying, "Now I understand perfectly."

Mike, our firefighter from chapter 2, understands his elephant; it craves achievement. The more I-did-this-today boxes he can tick off, the happier his elephant is.

Rob, the personal trainer, and Maya, the wellness instructor, each have an elephant that wants to hear a thank you from someone they have helped. That elephant will bring them back to work every day, to keep doing what they're doing, and gets a warm fuzzy feeling every time someone says to them, "You really helped me."

Want to be a good rider? Learn how to take care of your elephant.

Identify Your Strengths

The next step in your transition is for you to identify your strengths. What are your particular gifts? Which of your skills would you like to be able to use?

One of my skills is to be able to explain difficult concepts in simple terms. For years I taught non-technical people how to use computers. I taught law to non-lawyers and English as a Second Language to non-native speakers. When I use this skill in my teaching, I feel confident that people are getting a piece of my uniqueness, and that rewards me.

If you don't know your strengths, you need to spend time figuring them out. If you do know them, make a list and rank them in order of preference. You'll want to refer back to this list from time to time as you evaluate alternatives to you current situation.

Explore the possibilities

The next step is to explore the possibilities. Whether you want a different kind of job, a different career, or simply a different environment, you owe it to yourself to find out what is out there.

Maybe you want to be an entrepreneur, to run a large or small business. Maybe you want to be a consultant, working independently with a variety of jobs. Whatever it is, lots of resources are out there to help orient you.

Get a Coach

In chapter 10, I pointed out how senior management in the government tends to shun the use of executive coaches, which are standard practice for management in the Real World. For some reason, despite all the rhetoric in the government promoting training and continuous improvement, business coaching is seen as a luxury rather than a necessity,.

Unfortunately, that mindset has trickled down, and has biased the understanding of the value of coaching in the rank-and-file levels. Instead of associating individualized coaching with personal growth and customized advice, too many public servants think of it as a form of instructional training—or worse, remedial counselling. If you are one of them, it's time to change your mindset.

In the Real World, people of all sorts use coaches. Athletes at all levels, from the most competitive down

> A good coach can save you time, money, and effort.

to the weekend warrior, use a coach more commonly called a "personal trainer." Financial investors of all levels, from the most sophisticated down to the beginner, use a coach more commonly called a "financial advisor." Entrepreneurs at every level use business coaches; people needing help marketing their services use marketing coaches; and people seeking new careers use career coaches.

Personally, I can count at least three coaches that I use regularly in various areas of my life. I bring in others for short periods as and when I need them.

Don't be afraid to reach out to the right people for expertise. Even if you have to pay for it, as you do in many cases, it's well worth the money. The knowledge and experience a coach can bring you can save you hundreds of wasted hours, thousands of wasted dollars, and incalculable amounts of wasted energy and stress.

Acknowledging Other Priorities

I'll be the first to acknowledge that not everybody is in a position to spend time looking for other work. Sometimes other circumstances of your life take priority over taking time to choose your career.

For instance, you may be a full-time parent as well as a full-time employee, with three hungry mouths to feed at home and little other support. Perhaps you have a sick relative whose care takes up a lot of your energy, or you may be trying to cope with a personal health issue of your own.

In situations like these your mental health is paramount, and to the extent that leaving a secure position will compromise your mental health, it is not in your best interest.

Sometimes the tumult you experience in your daily life outside the office is so oppressive that the government office—stressful as it might be—becomes a welcome respite. The regularity of your schedule at work, the freedom from stresses at home, and the familiarity of old colleagues can be blessed relief from the disorder of a chaotic world. Sure, the job may not be right for you, but for a while the need to match your job to your passions must take a back seat to your need for a temporary escape from external pressures.

But only for a while. If this describes your life perpetually, you have a bigger problem that needs resolving sooner rather than later. In this case, you would be smart to seek professional help. There will come a time when you will retire for good, and it shouldn't be into a situation that's worse than your work life.

Go for it!

You deserve to love your work. I truly believe that. If you now believe that loving your work is a place you want to get to, then I have done my job. The rest is up to you.

Dream. Imagine. Fantasize.

Learn about your passions, your skills, and your personality, and how they all intertwine. This step is formally called *introspection*, but it doesn't need to be as solemn as it needs to be honest.

Explore. See what's out there. Even while you're in the introspection stage, you can find inspiration in things other people are doing.

Join a group. Hire a career or business coach. Visit some of the web sites dedicated to helping people like you get back on track.

Don't let old beliefs, fears, and doubts hold you back, and don't sabotage your efforts by assuming that nothing out there will be any different. You owe it to yourself at least to open your mind and investigate the possibilities.

You really can love your work. A whole wide world awaits you outside the public service.

Go find it.

Links to sources and other
resources are available on the
Unlocking the Golden Handcuffs web site
www.goldenhandcuffs.net/

ABOUT THE AUTHOR

 LEWIS EISEN

Lewis S. Eisen, B.A. J.D. C.I.P, obtained a law degree at the University of Toronto and practiced law in the same city for a few years. In 1986 he moved into the area of law office technology management, a field still in its infancy at the time. He worked with a variety of profit and nonprofit organizations, gaining extensive experience in the corporate support function.

From 2001 to 2017 he worked in the Government of Canada, pending the last few years specializing in developing administrative policies, mostly for the information management support function. He has written several books and dozens of articles for journals and newspapers, and speaks frequently at venues across the United States and Canada.

Combining his legal background with his knowledge of policy writing, Lewis runs workshops helping organizations improve their policy instruments by making them clearer, more succinct, and more respectful.

He is an avid fitness enthusiast, gardener and pet owner, and is currently based in Ottawa, Canada.

CPSIA information can be obtained
at www.ICGtesting.com
Printed in the USA
LVHW011205180119
604394LV00005B/126

9 781988 749037